AVOS D'REBBI NOSSON

אבות דרבי נתן

VOLUME I

Translated by
Rabbi Avraham Yaakov Finkel

YESHIVATH BETH MOSHE
SCRANTON, PA.

TABLE OF CONTENTS

VOLUME I

הקדמה
מראש הישיבה
מורינו הרב יעקב שניידמאן שליט"א

אמר רב יהודה האי מאן דבעי למהוי חסידא לקיים מילי דנזיקין
רבא אמר מילי דאבות ואמרי לה מילי דברכות (בבא קמא ל.) והנה
בפשוטו יש לפרש דעיקר תואר חסיד לדעת רבא נאמר על איש שלם
במדותיו בין אדם לחברו ובין אדם למקום ובא לשלמות זה על יד
קיום מילי דאבות. אמנם נראה דמוכרח לפרש ענין חסידות באופן
אחר מהא דאיתא באבות דרבי נתן וז"ל כשם שהצדיקים הראשונים
היו חסידים כך בהמתן היו חסידות. אמרו גמליו של אברהם אבינו
לא נכנסו לבית שיש בו עבודת אלילים שנאמר ואנכי פניתי הבית
ומקום לגמלים, ואנכי פניתי את הבית מתרפים ומה ת"ל ומקום
לגמלים מלמד שלא נכנסו לבית לבן הארמי עד שפנו כל העכ"א מפנ־
יהם עכ"ל. והרי אצל בהמה לא שייך לומר שהיא שלימה במדותיה
אלא נראה דחסיד היינו מי שהוא במדרגה שמקיים מעשה מצוות
וחיובי התורה בטבעו ובמדרגה זו כמעט א"א לו לעבור על מצות
הי"ת. ובאופן זה יתכן לומר על בהמות שהן חסידות, שמוטבע בטבען
שלא לעבור על המצוות. ועיין באורחות צדיקים פ"ג דכתב וז"ל
חסיד נקרא על שם הבושה כי חסיד לשון לבן הוא כי תרגומא של
החסידה הוא חוריתא (ויקרא יא, יט) וכן "ולא עתה פניו יחורו"
(ישעיה כט, כב) תרגום של חרפה הוא חסודא וכל זה למה כי החסיד
צריך לסבל בושה כדי לקיים את התורה וצריך להעביר מעל פניו
הבושה במקום מצוה ואז נקרא חסיד עכ"ל ונראה כוונתו כמו
שביארנו שמי שמקיים התורה בטבעו יסבל הבושה וחרפה כדי לקיים
התורה.

וביאר רבא דהדרך להגיע למדרגה זאת הוא ע"י קיום מילי
דאבות ונראה טעם הדבר דעיקר המפריע מעבודת ה' הוא מדות של
האדם וכמו שאמרו חז"ל ר' אלעזר הקפר אומר הקנאה והתאוה
והכבוד מוציאין את האדם מן העולם. וביאר במנורת המאור וז"ל כל
אחת משלש מדות הללו, הן מסבבות להפסיד אמונתו של האדם
וממיתות לו קדם זמנו וטורדין לו מן העולם הבא עכ"ל הרי מבואר
שמדות רעות אלו מפסידות אמונתו. והנה האדם שיש לו נשמה
טהורה מצד עצמו נוטה אחר עבודת ה' אך רוע המדות מסיתים אותו
לעזוב עבודת ה' עד שלבסוף יבא לידי כפירה ח"ו. וכן כתב הגאון ר'
אלחנן וסארמאן זצ"ל בספרו עקבתא דמשיחא דיש תביעה על כל
בנ"א שיאמינו בבורא עולם והקשה דאיך אפשר לתבוע אדם פשוט
שיהיה מאמין והרי גדולי חכמי אומות העולם נסתבכו בזה וכמה
מהם חברו חבורים להוכיח דהעולם קדמון וכופרים בבורא עולם
ותירץ דבאמת כל הספקות נולדים רק מרוע מדות האדם, ואלולא זה
היו הכל מודים בבורא ית' דהרי השמים מספרים כבוד אל. וכן הוא
בעניננו מי שמקיים מילי דאבות מסלק ממנו רוע המדות וממילא
מתבטלים רובא דרובא דפתויי היצר ונקל לו לעלות למדרגת חסיד
והיינו למדרגה שבטבעו עובד הי"ת בתכלית.

SUMMARY OF
RABBI YAAKOV SCHNAIDMAN'S
PROLOGUE

⸺⸺◉⸺⸺

R av Yehudah says, one who desires to be a chosid should be
meticulous in laws of monetary damages. Rava say he should
fulfill the words of Tractate Avos. Others say he should be meticulous about saying blessings (Baba Kama 30a).

Simply one would explain a chosid according to Rava, as one
who has attained perfection in his character traits both in his
relationship towards his fellow man and in his relationship with
heaven. However, it seems from Avos D'Rebbi Nosson that there
is a different interpretation, for it says, "Just as the pious ones of
old were chassidim so too, were their animals. Concerning the
camels of our forefather Avraham, it is said, that they would not
enter a home that contained idols." Since one cannot say that animals attain perfection in character development and fear of heaven,
calling them chassidim must mean that they reached a level that by
their very nature they want to do the mitzvos and obligations of
the Torah. Once one attains this level it is almost impossible for
him to sin.

One can infer this interpretation from the *Orchos Tzadikim* who
says the word chosid is related to the word shame, since chosid can
be translated as white and one must agree to become white with
shame in order to perform a mitzvah. One, who by his very nature
wants to do mitzvos, will certainly do them even if he is shamed
while doing them.

Rava explains that to reach this level one must study the Tractate
of Avos. It seems that the reason for this is, that the greatest hin-

Rabbi Yaakov Schnaidman is the Rosh Yeshivah of Yeshivath Beth Moshe —
Scranton, Pennsylvania.

drance to serving the Almighty comes through bad character traits as Rabbi Elozor Hakappar says, "Jealousy, desire, and honor remove a person from this world." The *Menoras Hameor* elaborates that these three character faults cause one to lose his faith, and lose his life in this world and the next. A man's soul is naturally pure, yearning to do the service of G-d, however his bad character traits lead him astray.

Rav Elchonon Wasserman ztz"l in his book, "The times of Moshiach", writes that everyone is obligated to believe in G-d. How is it possible for everyone to have such an obligation, when even great philosophers wrote books claiming the world always existed thus denying the Creator? He answers, that in fact everyone has the intellectual ability to recognize the Creator, for the heavens proclaim the honor of G-d, however his bad character traits misguide him leading him astray.

Rava teaches us that one who accepts the teachings of the Tractate of Avos, will refine his character traits, thereby becoming capable of withstanding most of the temptations of the Yetzer Hara, thus he will become a true chasid, who naturally wants to serve Hashem.

TRANSLATOR'S INTRODUCTION

⊷◉⊶

"Ethics of the Fathers According to Rabbi Nosson," better known as *Avos D'Rebbi Nosson* is a compilation of aggadic teachings of the Sages of the Gemara. It is one of the minor tractates of the Talmud printed in the same volume of the Gemara as *meseches Avodah Zarah*, immediately following *meseches Avos* the only tractate in the Talmud that deals exclusively with lessons of ethics and moral conduct.

Avos D'Rebbi Nosson expounds and elaborates on *meseches Avos*. While *meseches Avos* contains six chapters, *Avos D'Rebbi Nosson* comprises forty-one chapters, of which 20 chapters are included in this volume. It is a veritable treasure trove of profound ethical insights, fascinating anecdotes about the great Sages, and a wellspring of inspiring moral teachings.

To cite a few examples: The Mishnah in *Avos* 2:16 says: "A grudging eye, the evil impulse, and hatred of other people put a man out of the world."

Comments *Avos D'Rebbi Nosson* (chapter 16): How does one avoid a grudging eye? Just as a man is happy when things go well for him, so should he be happy when things go well for his neighbor. And just as a man hates if his wife and children are maligned, so should he hate it if his neighbor's wife and children are maligned.

The Mishnah in *Avos* 1:4 says: "You should thirstily drink in the words of the Sages." To illustrate this adage, *Avos D'Rebbi Nosson* relates the moving story of Rabbi Akiva's meteoric rise from ignorant shepherd to illustrious Torah giant.

In *Avos D'Rebbi Nosson* we find numerous sayings of the Sages that are not mentioned anywhere else in the Gemara or Midrash. For example, Chapter 12 offers a poignant description of the death of Moshe Rabbeinu, and how the angel of death vainly searched for Moshe's soul.

It is unclear who compiled *Avos D'Rebbi Nosson*. The work is generally attributed to Rabbi Nosson HaBavli, a tanna of the fourth generation, teacher of Rabbi Eliezer, Rabbi Tarfon and Rabbi Yishmael (*Shabbos* 12b). Rabbi Yehudah Hanassi, the compiler of the Mishnah, received many teachings from Rabbi Nosson and often disputed his opinion (*Bava Basra* 131a). Rabbi Nosson is mentioned also in *Bava Kamma* 53a and *Kesubos* 19a. The Gemara in *Gittin* 70a relates that Eliyahu Hanavi appeared to Rabbi Nosson.

Some say that Rabbi Nosson did not compile the entire tractate, rather *Avos D'Rebbi Nosson* derives its name from the fact that Rabbi Nosson is quoted in the first mishnah.

Numerous commentaries have been written on *Avos D'Rebbi Nosson*. Prominent among these are: *Binyan Yehoshua* by Rabbi Yehoshua Falk (Durenfurth, 1788), *Ben Avraham* by Rabbi Eliyahu Mideliatitz (Vilna, 1833), and *Sh'nei Eliyahu* by the Vilna Gaon (Vilna, 1833) in which the Gaon corrects the numerous errors that crept into the text.

A brief introduction such as this cannot begin to do justice to a monumental classic like *Avos D'Rebbi Nosson*. One has to delve into the words of the Sages to get an inkling of the towering greatness of these spiritual giants. By studying their teachings in depth one is uplifted and inspired to follow their guidance. It is my hope that this translation will open a window on the profound wisdom of the *chachmei HaTalmud*, and help in disseminating their teachings, *lehagdil Torah ulehadirah*, "that the Torah be made great and glorious."

AVRAHAM YAAKOV FINKEL
Tamuz, 5766/06

AVOS D'REBBI NOSSON

אבות דרבי נתן

VOLUME I

CHAPTER ONE

MOSHE IN THE HEAVENLY CLOUD

1. Moshe [went up Mount Sinai] in a Heavenly cloud. He was covered by and[1] sanctified in the cloud in order to receive the Torah from [Hashem at] Sinai, as it says, *The glory of Hashem rested on Mount Sinai, and the cloud covered him for six days* (*Shemos* 24:16), covering Moshe, to purify him. According to R. Yose Hagelili, this took place *after* the giving of the Ten Commandments.

R. Akiva, on the other hand, says, the verse [is to be translated as,] *And the cloud covered it*[2] *for six days* referring to the mountain and not to Moshe. [Moshe had not yet gone up the mountain, and the six days are counted] from the beginning of the month Sivan [i.e., *before* the giving of the Ten Commandments]. [Then it says,] *On the seventh day, He called to Moshe from the midst of the cloud.* [Moshe was standing at the bottom of the mountain together with all Yisrael, and G-d spoke to the entire nation. If all Yisrael were present, why does the verse say,] G-d called to Moshe, rather than all the people? Moshe was singled out in order to honor him.

R. Nosson [who agrees with R. Yose Hagelili that the cloud covered Moshe] said: Why was Moshe made to wait six days [in the Heavenly cloud] before G-d spoke to him? In order to dissolve all the food and drink in his intestines, sanctifying him, and mak-

---

[1]   The Gra's version, following the text of *Yoma* 4a.
[2]   The verse uses the Hebrew *Veyechaseihu* which may be translated "covered him" or "covered it".

ing him like one of the ministering angels.

R. Masya b. Cheresh [who also agrees with R. Yose Hagelili] said: The purpose of Moshe's six days of separation was to fill him with awe, so he would receive the words of the Torah with awe, fear, trembling, and trepidation. For it says, *Serve Hashem with awe, and rejoice with trembling* (*Tehillim* 2:11).

TORAH STUDY AND WORLDLY PURSUITS

R. Yoshiah and R. Masya b. Cheresh were [study partners] who learned together. One day R. Yoshiah left [the yeshivah] to go into business. Said R. Masya b. Cheresh to him, "Rebbi, why do you set aside the words of the living G-d to become involved in worldly pursuits? Although you are my rebbi[3] and I am your student, I am telling you it is not good to set aside the words of the living G-d to devote yourself to worldly pursuits."

It was said of them: While they learned Torah they seemed to fight with each other, but they parted amiable as boyhood friends.

THE CHAIN OF TORAH TRADITION

2. The Torah was given at Sinai through Moshe, as it says, *He wrote [these words] on two stone tablets and gave them to me* (*Devarim* 5:19). And it says, *These are the decrees, laws and codes that Hashem set between Himself and B'nei Yisrael at Mount Sinai through the hand of Moshe* (*Vayikra* 26:46). The Torah that the Holy One, blessed be He, gave to Yisrael was given through the hands of Moshe alone, as it says, *Between Himself and B'nei Yisrael.* Moshe merited to be the emissary between G-d and *B'nei Yisrael.*

Moshe officiated during the seven days of the inauguration [of

---

[3] He called him *rebbi* out of humility; they were in fact study partners (*Ben Avraham*)

the Communion Tent], preparing the anointing oil, with which he anointed Aharon and his sons during these seven days of inauguration, and from which all later High Priests and kings were anointed. Elazar burned the red cow of the purification offering; and with [those ashes] the unclean were made clean throughout the generations.

Aharon and his sons were anointed with special anointing oil, as it says, *You must anoint Aharon and his sons, sanctifying them as priests to Me* (*Shemos* 30:30). R. Elazar explained: The anointing [of Aharon and his sons] was of overriding importance, indeed because of his anointing, later generations did not have to have to be anointed.[4]

3. Yehoshua received the Torah from Moshe, as it says, *Invest him [Yehoshua] with some of your splendor, so that the entire community of Yisrael will obey him* (*Bamidbar* 27:20).

The Elders received the Torah from Yehoshua, as it says, *The people served Hashem all the days of Yehoshua and all the days of the elders who outlived Yehoshua, who had seen all the great work of Hashem which He had done for Yisrael* (*Shofetim* 2:7).

The Judges received the Torah from the Elders, as it says, *It happened in the days when judges judged* [after the Elders had ceased to be the leaders] (*Ruth* 1:1).

The Prophets received the Torah from the Judges, as it says, *I sent to you all My servants, the prophets, daily, rising early and sending them forth* (*Yirmeyah* 7:25).

SAYINGS OF THE MEN OF THE GREAT ASSEMBLY

Chaggai, Zechariah, and Malachi received the Torah from the Prophets. The Men of the Great Assembly[5] received the Torah

---

4 By contrast, kings and High Priests required anointing (*Shenei Eliyahu*).
5 A group of 120 sages who led the Jewish people at the beginning of the second Beis Hamikdash era. Included among them were Ezra, Mordechai, Chaggai, Zechariah, and Malachi.

from Chaggai, Zechariah, and Malachi. They said three things: Be cautious in judgment, raise many disciples, and make a [protective] fence for the Torah.

4. How should one "Be cautious in judgment"? Take time when sitting in judgment, since a judge who is not hasty is coolheaded in judgment, as it says, *These, too, are the proverbs of King Shlomoh, sheheeteeku—which were copied by—the men of Chizkiah, king of Yehudah (Mishlei* 25:1). Do not translate [sheheeteeku] as "they copied the proverbs"; rather understand it to mean they took their time[6] interpreting the meanings. Abba Shaul said: It does not mean they took their time, rather, they interpreted the text,[7] since originally, [the authorities] had decreed that the Books of *Mishlei, Shir Hashirim* and *Koheles* be concealed rather than included in the Books of *Tanach* because they are parables. They remained concealed until the men of Chizkiah[8] interpreted them.

For example, [in *Mishlei*] we find the following parable: *I looked out from the window of my house, and saw among the simple, noticed among the youths, a lad devoid of sense. He was crossing the street near her corner, walking toward her house, in the dusk of the evening, in the dark hours of the night. A woman comes toward him, dressed like a harlot, and with siege in her heart. She is bustling and restive; she is never at home. Now in the street, now in the square, she lurks at every corner. She lays hold of him and kisses him. Brazenly she says to him, "I vowed to bring a peace offering; Today I fulfilled my vows. Therefore I have come out to you, seeking you, and have found you. I have decked my couch with covers of dyed Egyptian linen; I have sprinkled my bed with myrrh, aloes, and cinnamon. Let us drink our fill of love till morning; Let us delight in amorous embrace. For [my] hus-*

---

6   The word *sheheeteeku* which means copied can also be translated as a form of *asak* meaning old representing a passage of time.

7   When one copies or transfers text he explains it.

8   The texts that reads "The Men of the Great Assembly" is an error, since Abba Shaul is referring to the men of Chizkiah (*Ben Avraham*)

band is away; He is off on a distant journey. He took his bag of money with him, and will return only at the set time" (*Mishlei* 7:7-20). [The sages explain that this refers to Potifar's wife attempting to seduce Yosef.]

And in *Shir Hashirim* it says, *Come my beloved, Let us go into the open; Let us lodge in the villages. Let us go early to the vineyards, Let us see if the vine has budded, If its blossoms have opened, If the pomegranates are in bloom. There I will give my love to you* (*Shir Hashirim* 7:12,13). [The sages interpret that this passage refers to the study of Torah].

And in *Koheles* it says, *O Youth, enjoy yourself while you are young! Let your heart lead you to enjoyment in the days of your youth. Follow the desires of your heart, And the glances of your eyes. But know well that G-d will call you to account, For all such things* (*Koheles* 11:9). [The sages explain that the fist half of this verse refers to the words of the Evil Inclination, while the latter half refers to the words of the good inclination].

Which proves, not that they took their time, but that they interpreted the text.

DO NOT SPEAK IN ANGER

"Be cautious in judgment," also means, to wait before you speak, carefully considering what you will say and not speaking in anger, for whoever speaks in anger forgets what he has to say. This happened to Moshe who forgot what he had to tell *B'nei Yisrael* when he spoke in anger. For it says, *Elazar the priest said to the soldiers returning from the campaign; This the rule that Hashem commanded Moshe* (*Bamidbar* 31:21). [Elazar implied: It is Moshe whom Hashem commanded, but he forgot the laws he had to convey to the people].[9]

---

[9] The laws of koshering utensils should have been transmitted to the people by Moshe rather than Elazar, but because Moshe became angry he forgot them (*Rashi*).

BILAM'S MALICIOUS ADVICE

Where do we find Moshe speaking in anger? When the officers returned from the military campaign [against Midian], *Moshe was angry at the officers: "Why have you kept all the women alive," Moshe demanded. "These [women] are exactly the ones who were involved with B'nei Yisrael at Bilam's instigation, causing them to be unfaithful to Hashem in the Pe'or incident, and bringing a plague on Hashem's community"* (*Bamidbar* 31:15,16).

To what does "*at Bilam's instigation*" refer to? It refers to the advice the wicked Bilam gave against Yisrael, as it says, [Bilam said to Balak,] *Now I am returning to my people, but first I will advise you about what this nation will do to your people in the final days* (*Bamidbar* 24:14). Bilam told Balak: "This nation which you hate is hungry and thirsty. They have nothing to eat and drink except manna. Set up booths stocked with food and drink for them, and place beautiful royal women in them to seduce the people to stray after Baal Pe'or. In this way they will fall by the hand of G-d". Balak immediately did all that the wicked Bilam told him to do. Now see what the wicked Bilam brought on Yisrael! 24,000 of them fell, as it says, *In that plague, 24,000 people perished* (*Bamidbar* 25:9). [Therefore, Moshe's anger at the officers for keeping the captured Moabite women alive was justified. Nevertheless, because he spoke in anger he forgot what he had to say.]

Surely a logical conclusion can be drawn from this: If Moshe our Teacher, the wisest of the wise, the greatest of all prophets, forgot what he had to say when he spoke in anger, how much more so shall we forget. This teaches one to be prudent in his speech, not speaking in anger.

A Fence For the Torah

5. Ben Azzai says: Choose your words carefully so you will not cause people to stumble; and make a fence for your words[10] the way G-d made a fence for His words. Adam too, made a fence for his words. The Torah made a fence for its words, and Moshe made a fence for his words. Iyov, the Prophets, the Writings, and the Sages, all made a fence for their words.

A Fence For G-d's Words

What fence did the Holy One, blessed be He, make for His words? [Referring to the destruction of Eretz Yisrael], it says, *All the nations will ask, "Why did Hashem do this to the land?"* (*Devarim* 29:23). This teaches, that it was obvious to G-d that future generations would ask this question. Therefore, He said to Moshe, "Moshe, write down [the following answer], leaving it for the coming generations, *They will say, "It is because they abandoned the covenant that Hashem, the G-d of their fathers made with them . . . They went and served foreign gods, bowing down to them. These gods were alien to them, something that was not their portion"* (*Devarim* 29:24,25). G-d made a fence around His words by writing in the Torah that people will recognize that G-d gave His creatures exactly what they deserve. [This verse is the "fence", for it precludes people from saying that calamities happen by chance rather than as Divine punishment.]

The Fence For Adam's Words

What fence did Adam make for his words? It says, *G-d gave the man a commandment, saying, "You may definitely eat from every tree of the garden. But from the Tree of Knowledge of good and evil, do not eat, for on the day that you eat from it, you will definitely die"*

---

10   Enact preventive measurements to safeguard the laws of the Torah.

(*Bereishis* 2:16,17). Adam, however, did not repeat the law to Chavah the way G-d said it to him, telling her instead, *But of the fruit of the tree that is in the middle of the garden, G-d said, "Do not eat it, and do not [even] touch it, or else you will die"* (*Bereishis* 3:3). By adding [the words, *do not touch it*] to G-d's prohibition, he made a fence for his words, wishing to safeguard himself and Chavah from even touching the tree.

At that point the evil serpent reasoned: Since I cannot make Adam stumble I will entrap Chavah. Sitting beside her, he talked with her at length, saying, "You tell me G-d commanded us not to touch the tree, yet, I am touching it, and I am not dying! Go ahead and touch it; you will not die either." What did the evil serpent do? Rising, he touched the tree with his hands and feet, shaking it until its fruits fell to the ground.

When the tree saw him it cried out, "O wicked one, wicked one, do not touch me!" as it says, *Let not the foot of arrogance come to me, and let not the hand of the wicked move me* (*Tehillim* 36:12).

6. Another explanation of the verse: *Let not the foot of arrogance come to me* refers to the wicked Titus—may his bones be crushed—for [when he destroyed the Beis Hamikdash] he kept striking the altar with his stick, shouting, "Lukos! Lukos![11] You are a king, and I am a king; come and wage war with me! How many oxen have been slaughtered on you, how many birds have been killed on you, how many wines have been poured out on you, how much incense has been burned on you! You are the one that destroys the whole world!" As it says, *O Ariel, Ariel,[12] city where David camped! You add [sins] year after year, until your holidays will be terminated* (*Yeshayah* 29:1).

The serpent continued: "You tell me G-d commanded us not to eat [from the tree], yet I am eating from it and I am not dying! Go ahead and eat from it; you will not die either." What did Chavah say

---

[11] "Wolf, Wolf!" using a derisive name for the altar.

[12] Ariel is the name of the altar in the Beis Hamikdash (see *Yechezkel* ch.43). The prophet is bemoaning the altar which will be destroyed by Titus.

to herself? "All the things which my master warned me about are false," for at first Chavah called Adam "my master." Immediately she took some of the fruit and ate it. She then gave some of the fruit to Adam and he ate it, as it says, *The woman saw that the tree was good to eat and desirable to the eyes . . . She took some of its fruit and ate [it]. She also gave some to her husband, and he ate [it]* (*Bereishis* 3:6).

CHAVAH'S CURSES

7. At that time Chavah was cursed with ten curses, as it says, *To the woman He said, "I will greatly increase your anguish and your pregnancy. It will be with anguish that you will give birth to children. Your passion will be to your husband, and he will dominate you* (*Bereishis* 3:16).

I will greatly increase (harbah arbe) refers to the two blood discharges: the blood of menstrual pain (1) and the blood of virginal pain (2).

your anguish refers to the pain of child rearing (3).

and your pregnancy refers to pregnancy pain (4).

It will be with anguish that you give birth to children is self-understood (5).

Your passion will be to your husband teaches that a woman longs for her husband when he is away on a trip (6).

And he will dominate you—for a man expresses his desire openly, but a woman solicits in her heart (7), her head covered like a mourner (8), as though she were locked up in prison (9) and banned from all men (10).

ADAM WENT TO EXTREMES

What prompted Chavah to touch the tree? The fence that Adam made for his words [forbidding even touching the tree] prompted her. Therefore the Rabbis said: Make a fence for your words, but do not go to extremes, because you will not be able to live up to your words if you overdo it. In the same vein, the Rabbis said: One should not add to what he has heard.

Rabbi Yose says: Better a standing fence that is ten handbreadths high than a fence a hundred cubits high which has fallen down.

THE SERPENT'S PLAN

What did the wicked serpent have in mind? He thought: I will kill Adam and marry his wife. Then I will be king over the whole world; I will walk upright and eat all the world's delicacies. Said the Holy One, blessed be He, to the serpent: "You intended to kill Adam and marry his wife; therefore, *I will plant hatred between you and the woman* (*Bereishis* 3:15). You intended to be king over the whole world; therefore, *Cursed are you more than all the livestock* (*Bereishis* 3:14). You intended to walk upright; therefore, *On your belly you shall crawl* (3:14). You intended to eat all the world's delicacies; therefore, *Dust you shall eat all the days of your life*" (3:14).

LOSS OF A GREAT SERVANT

R. Shimon b. Menasia says: What a pity that a great servant was lost to the world, for had the serpent not been cursed, every Jew would have had two serpents in his house, sending one to the east and one to the west to bring him precious gems, costly pearls and every kind of precious article in the world. No creature could have harmed the [serpents]. Furthermore, they would have been used instead of camels, donkeys or mules, to haul manure to the gardens and orchards.

8. R. Yehudah b. Beseirah says: Adam sat comfortably in Gan Eden while the ministering angels roasted meat[13] and cooled wine before him. When the serpent looked in and saw his glory, he became envious.

---

[13] This was meat that came down from heaven, since eating meat was permitted only after the days of Noach (*Sanhedrin* 59b).

THE CREATION OF ADAM

How was Adam created? In the first hour Adam's dust was collected; in the second, it was kneaded into a shapeless mass; in the third his limbs were shaped and his orifices were opened; in the fourth, a soul was infused into him; in the fifth, he stood up on his feet; in the sixth, he named all the animals; in the seventh, Chavah became his bride; in the eighth, they went to bed as two people, and left the bed as four [Cain and his twin sister were born]; in the ninth, he entered Gan Eden; in the tenth, he was commanded [not to eat from the Tree]; in the eleventh, he transgressed; in the twelfth, he was driven out of Gan Eden, as it says, *As for man, he does not lodge overnight in glory* (*Tehillim* 49:13) [meaning, Adam, remained in grandeur in Gan Eden only the first day, but did not stay overnight.]

THE *SONG* OF THE DAY

What psalm [did the Levites] say on the first day of the week [during the offering of the regular morning sacrifice]?—[The psalm beginning with the verse,] *The earth is Hashem's and its fullness* (*Tehillim* 24). Why this psalm? Because [on that day] G-d created the world, in order to give it to man, and He alone ruled over the world.

What did they say on the second day of the week?—[The psalm beginning with the verse,] *Great is Hashem and much praised in the city of our G-d, Mount of His holiness* (*Tehillim* 48). Why this psalm? Because [on the second day of Creation] G-d divided His works [between the heavenly and the earthly components of the universe] and reigned over both.

On the third day they said, [the psalm beginning with the verse], *G-d stands in the Divine assembly, in the midst of judges shall He judge* (*Tehillim* 82), because on the third day of Creation, G-d revealed the earth in His wisdom and prepared dry land for His community. [The continued existence of the world depends on the maintenance of justice and equity. Therefore the psalm speaks of justice (*Maharsha*).]

On the fourth day they said, *O G-d of vengeance, Hashem!* (*Tehillim* 94), because [on the fourth day of Creation], G-d created the sun, the moon, the stars and the zodiac [which man came to regard as gods to be worshipped]. [G-d is called "*G-d of vengeance*"] for in the future He will punish those who worship the luminaries.

On the fifth day they said, *Sing joyously to the G-d of our might* (*Tehillim* 81), because [on the fifth day of Creation], G-d created fish and birds [whose beauty and colorful variety inspire people] to praise His name.

On the sixth day they said, *Hashem is King, He is robed in grandeur* (*Tehillim* 93), because [on the sixth day] He completed His works and reigned over them.

On the seventh day they said, *A psalm, a song for the Shabbos day* (*Tehillim* 92). [The psalm does not refer to Shabbos, rather it refers to the World to Come, when the world will be all Shabbos, for the world as we know it will come to an end and be destroyed before the resurrection of the dead (Rashi)]. In the new world there will be neither eating, drinking nor business. Rather, the righteous will sit with crowns on their heads enjoying the radiance of the *Shechinah*, just like ministering angels, as it says, *They gazed at G-d, yet they ate and drank* (*Shemos* 24:11.

Why was Adam was created on the eve of Shabbos? So he might go immediately to his Shabbos meal.

Two Parables

R. Shimon b. Elazar says: Let me compare Adam to this parable. A man married a convert,[14] warning her, "My dear, don't eat bread with unclean hands, don't eat fruits that have not been tithed,

---

[14] Symbolizing Chavah who did not know what G-d had commanded Adam.

don't desecrate the Shabbos, don't carelessly make vows, and don't keep company with other men. If you do any of these things you will surely die." Another man [i.e., the serpent] ate bread with unclean hands in her presence, ate fruits which had not been tithed, desecrated the Shabbos, carelessly made vows, and kept company with her. What did the convert think? All the things my husband warned me about are false. She immediately transgressed them all.

R. Shimon b. Yocha'i says: Let me compare Adam to this parable. A man had a wife at home [i.e. Chavah in Gan Eden]. What did he do? He filled a jar with choice figs and nuts, placed a scorpion, [on top], sealed the jar with a tight-fitting lid, and put it in a corner. "My dear," he told his wife, "you may have everything you want in this house, except this jar. Don't even touch it." What did the wife do? As soon as her husband left for the market, she opened the jar and stuck her hand inside. Stung by the scorpion, she staggered and collapsed on her bed. Returning from the market, the husband cried out, "What happened!" She replied, "When I put my hand in the jar, a scorpion stung me, and now I am dying!" He scolded her, "Didn't I tell you from the start, that you may have everything in this house, except this jar, which you may not even touch." Fuming with anger, he sent her away.

The two parables apply to Adam. G-d told him, *You may definitely eat from every tree in the garden. But from the Tree of Knowledge of good and evil, do not eat from it, for on the day you eat from it, you will definitely die* (*Bereishis* 2:16,17). When he ate from it, he was expelled, as it says, *As for man, he does not lodge overnight in glory; he is like the beasts that perish* (*Tehillim* 49:13) [meaning, Adam remained in grandeur in Gan Eden only the first day, but did not stay overnight].

THE CREATION OF ADAM

On the day [Adam was created, the dust from which he was created] was [loosely] laid out in the form of a man; on that day [the dust] was kneaded into a dough-like mass; on that day his limbs were attached and his orifices were opened; on that day a soul was infused into him; on that day he stood up on his feet; on that day he named [all the animals]; on that day Chavah became his bride; on that day they went to bed as two people, and got up as four [Cain and his twin sister were born]. Rabbi Yehudah b. Beseirah says: On that day they went to bed as two people, and got up as seven [Adam, Chavah, Cain and his twin, and Hevel and his two twins.][15] On that day he entered Gan Eden; on that day he was commanded [not to eat from the Tree]; on that day he transgressed, and on that day he was driven out of Gan Eden.

ADAM AND CHAVAH'S THREE PUNISHMENTS

On that day three[16] decrees were pronounced against Adam, as it says, *To Adam He said, "Because you listened to your wife . . . therefore the ground is cursed because of you. (1) You will derive food from it with anguish . . . (2) It will bring forth thorns and thistles for you,* and (3) *you will eat the grass of the field"* (*Bereishis* 3:17,18).

When Adam heard G-d say to him, *And you will eat the grass of the field,* he trembled with all his limbs [a sign that he repented of his sin]. He said to G-d, "Master of the universe! Will I and my donkey eat from the same trough?" Replied G-d, "Because you trembled with all your limbs [showing true remorse], *By the sweat of your brow you will eat bread,* [and not grass]" (*Bereishis* 3:19).

Just as three decrees were pronounced against Adam, so were three decrees pronounced against Chavah, as it says, *I will greatly increase your anguish and your pregnancy. It will be in anguish that you will give birth to children. Your passion will be to your husband, and he will dominate you* (*Bereishis* 3:16).

I will greatly implies that at the beginning of her period a woman is in pain.

---

15 *Ben Avraham, Binyan Yehoshua,* see *Tosafos, Sanhedrin* 38b.
16 The Gra's emendation: ten decrees, based on *Zohar Ruth.*

Increase implies that a woman's first sexual intercourse is painful.

Your anguish and your pregnancy implies that during the first three months of pregnancy a woman looks pale and unattractive.

ADAM'S SACRIFICE

Toward evening [of Adam's first day], seeing the world gradually growing dark, Adam said: "Woe is me! Because of my sin, G-d is plunging the world into darkness." He did not know that this was the natural way of the world. The next morning, noticing the sun rising in the east he was extremely happy. Quickly he built an altar and offered an ox whose horns preceded its hoofs,[17] as it says, *It shall please Hashem more than a full-grown bull with horns and hoofs* (*Tehillim* 69:32).

The ox which Adam offered, the bull which Noach offered, and the ram which Avraham offered on the altar instead of his son, as it says, *Avraham then looked up and saw a ram caught by its horns in the thicket* (*Bereishis* 22:13), all had horns that preceded their hoofs.[18]

At that time [on Shabbos morning when Adam brought the sacrifice], three groups of ministering angels came down holding lutes, lyres and all kinds of musical instruments. They joined Adam in singing songs of praise, as it says, *A psalm, a song for the Shabbos day. It is good to thank Hashem, and to sing praise to Your name, O Exalted One. To relate Your kindness in the morning and Your faith in the nights* (*Tehillim* 92:1-3).

To relate your kindness in the morning—refers to the World to Come which is compared to the morning, as it says, *They are new every morning; great is Your faithfulness* (*Eichah* 3:23).[19]

---

[17] All animals were created in their mature form; an ox with full-grown horns. And since the head was created first, the horns preceded the hoofs (*Rashi, Avodah Zarah* 8a).

[18] They were all created on the eve of Shabbos of Creation.

[19] The renewal of creation we see every morning tells us that You are faithful to revive the dead in the World to Come (*Bereishis Rabbah* 48)

Your faith in the nights—refers to this world which is compared to the nights, as it says, *The Dumah Pronouncement. A call comes to me from Seir, "Watchman, what of the night? Watchman, what of the night?"* (*Yeshayah* 31:11).[20]

THE CURSE OF THE SERPENT

At that time [when G-d wanted to pronounce Adam's punishment] the Holy One, blessed be He, said: "If I do not punish the serpent first, I will be destroying the whole world."[21] He continued: "I made [Adam] king over the whole world. How could he have gone wrong, eating from the fruit of the Tree!" But [realizing that it was the serpent that seduced Chavah,] G-d immediately turned to the serpent and cursed him [first], as it says, *G-d said to the serpent . . . cursed are you* (*Bereishis* 3:14). Rabbi Yose says: Had the serpent's curse been written after the curses of Adam and Chavah, the world would have been destroyed.

When the Holy One, blessed be He, created Adam, He formed him with two faces, one in front and one in back, as it says, *Back and front have You formed me, and You have laid Your hand upon me* (*Tehillim* 139:5). [Awed by Adam's exalted appearance] the ministering angels came down to serve him, but G-d took him and placed him under His wings, as it says, *You have laid Your hand upon me.*

---

20   Yisrael cries out to G-d: "When will the *galus* end in this world that is like a long night?" (*Ben Avraham*).

21   Had G-d placed the full blame for the sin on Adam, He would have had to destroy the whole world. By judging the serpent first, G-d holds it responsible for the transgression. Thus Adam's guilt is mitigated and the world is not destroyed (*Ben Avraham*).

Adam and the Beis Hamikdash Created With G-d's Two Hands

Another interpretation of, *You have laid Your hand upon me*: When Adam sinned, the Holy One, blessed be He, removed one of His hands. We derive that Adam and the Beis Hamikdash were created with both of G-d's hands. From what verse do we know that Adam was created with both of G-d's hands? It says, *Your hands made me and prepared me* (*Tehillim* 119:73). From what verse do we know that the Beis Hamikdash was created with both of G-d's hands? It says, *The shrine of Hashem, Your hands have founded* (*Shemos* 15:17). And it says, *And He brought them to His sacred boundary, this mountain that His right hand acquired* (*Tehillim* 78:54), and, *Hashem will reign forever and ever* (*Shemos* 15:18).[22]

CHAPTER TWO

The Fence for the Torah

1.   What is the [preventive] fence the Torah made for its words? It says, *Do not come close to a woman who is ritually unclean because of her menstruation* (*Vayikra* 18:19). You may think her husband may hug and kiss her or engage her in frivolous chitchat [during her menstruation]. To teach you otherwise it says, *Do not come close.* You may think he can sleep with her on the bed while she is dressed. The Torah says, *Do not come close.* May she wash her face and paint her eyes? The Torah says, *Concerning a woman who*

---

[22] This verse is used to conclude the chapter.

suffers through her separation (*Vayikra* 15:33)—throughout all the days of her menstruation she should be separated [and not make herself attractive to her husband]. Therefore, the Rabbis thought highly of a woman who did not beautify herself during her monthly period, and were displeased with a woman who primped and beautified herself during her monthly period.

2. A Torah scholar who had learned a great deal of Mishnah and Gemara and had served the Torah scholars died in the prime of life. His wife took his *tefillin* and carried them around to the synagogues and the *batei midrash*, crying to the rabbis: "It is written in the Torah, '*This [i.e., the Torah] is your life and the length of your days*' (*Devarim* 30:20). My husband learned a great deal of Mishnah and Gemara and served many scholars. Why did he die in the prime of life?" No one could answer her.

Once she met Eliyahu the prophet. "My daughter why are you crying so bitterly?" he asked her. She told him the tragic story.

Eliyahu said to her, "My daughter! How did he conduct himself during your *niddah* period [when a woman is forbidden to her husband]?"

She replied, "God forbid! He did not even touch me with his little finger."

"And how did he relate to you during your "days of white garments"? [After the flow has ended a woman puts on fresh white garments and examines herself for seven days to make sure that no stains are found. During those seven days she is also forbidden to her husband.]

She answered, "He ate and drank together with me, and he slept together with me, but it did not enter his mind to have marital relations." [He did not act properly, for the laws of separation apply when a woman is counting her seven clean days just as they apply when she is actually menstruating.]

Said Eliyahu, "Blessed be G-d for slaying him [because he did not show proper respect for the Torah law]. For it says, *[A man should] not come close to a woman who is ritually unclean because of her men-*

struation, [both during the days of her menstrual flow and at any time before she counted the full seven days and immersed in the *mikveh*].

SAFEGUARDS

Another example of a fence for the Torah: The Torah says, *No person shall approach a close relative to commit a sexual offense* (*Vayikra* 18:6). Therefore, the Rabbis decreed [as a safeguard] that a man should not be alone in an inn with any woman, even his sister or daughter, because of what people might think. [Not realizing she is his relative, they may suspect him of immorality]. Neither should a man talk or walk in the street, with his wife, much less another woman, because of what people may think.

[Regarding incest] it says, *A man shall not approach* (*Vayikra* 18:6), and [concerning a menstruating woman] it says, *You shall not approach* (*Vayikra* 18:19). Thus, we learn to keep away from anything which may lead to transgression; one must keep away from things that are loathsome and from things that seem loathsome. Therefore the Sages said: Stay away from a minor sin so you will not be drawn to a grave sin. Run to perform an easy mitzvah for it will lead you to a major mitzvah.

[The Sages interpret the verse,] *Your belly is like a heap of wheat hedged about with lilies* (*Shir Hashirim* 7:3) as follows: *Your belly is like a heap of wheat* refers the community of Yisrael. *Hedged about with lilies* refers to the seventy Elders [of the Sanhedrin[23] who erect hedges to safeguard the laws of the Torah].

"EASY" AND "DIFFICULT" MITZVOS

Another interpretation: *Your belly is like a heap of wheat* refers to the difficult mitzvos. *Hedged about with lilies* refers to the easy mitzvos which are tender like lilies. By observing [all the mitzvos] Yisrael merits [everlasting] life in the World to Come. Why? A

---

[23] The Sanhedrin actually had 71 members.

man's menstruating wife is at home with him. If he wishes, he may have relations with her, and if he wishes he will not have relations with her. Does anyone see him? Can anyone tell him what to do? He fears only The One who prohibited contact when his wife is a *niddah* until she immerses.

This is also true about the law of separating *challah,*[24] and the law of "the first of your shearing" [i.e., the first wool of one's sheep must be given to the kohen. In both cases, no one knows whether one separated *challah* or gave the first of his shearing]. The performance of these easy mitzvos, which are tender like lilies, will lead Yisrael to life in the World to Come.

MOSHE ACTING ON HIS OWN INITIATIVE

3. What fence did Moshe make for his words? It says, [Before the Giving of the Torah,] *Hashem said to Moshe, "Go to the people, and sanctify them today and tomorrow"* (*Shemos* 19:10). The righteous Moshe did not speak to the people the way G-d had spoken to him. Instead, he said to them: *Keep yourselves in readiness for three days. Do not come near a woman* (*Shemos* 19:15). On his own initiative, Moshe added one day for their sake. He said: If a man has intercourse with his wife and on the third day semen flows from her, they will be unclean; in that case the women will receive the Torah from Mount Sinai in impurity. Therefore, I will add a day, so no man will have intercourse with his wife, and no semen will be discharged, and they will be clean.

This is one of the things which Moshe did on his own account, and G-d agreed with him. [But there were also other cases where he acted on his own account:] He broke the tablets [on his own account] and G-d agreed with his action. He stayed away from the Communion Tent [on his own accord],[25] and G-d agreed with his action. He stayed away from his wife [on his own initiative], and G-d agreed with his course of action.

---

24 *Bamidbar* 15:17-21. A gift to the Kohen that must be separated from dough.
25 This will be explained shortly.

MOSHE STAYED AWAY FROM HIS WIFE

Moshe stayed away from his wife, and G-d agreed with his course of action. Why? He reasoned: B'nei Yisrael were sanctified only for the short time it took to receive the Ten Commandments from Mount Sinai, yet G-d told me, *Go to the people, and sanctify them today and tomorrow . . . Do not come near a woman* (*Shemos* 19:10). I do not know when G-d will speak to me, whether during the day or at night; I must be ready every hour of every day, so surely I should stay away from my wife! And G-d agreed with his decision.

R. Yehudah b. Beseirah says: Moshe stayed away from his wife only after being told by G-d, as it says, *With him I speak mouth to mouth* (*Bamidbar* 12:8)—mouth to mouth I told him: "Keep away from your wife," and he stayed away.

Some say: Moshe stayed away from his wife only after being told by G-d, as it says: [After the Ten Commandments, Hashem said to Moshe,] *Go tell them: Return to your tents* (*Devarim* 5:27) [a euphemism for marital relations] which is followed by, *You, however, must remain here with Me* (*Devarim* 5:28). [Having told B'nei Yisrael to return to their tents,] Moshe went back and kept away from his wife, and G-d agreed with his decision.

MOSHE STAYED AWAY FROM THE COMMUNION TENT

Moshe stayed away from the Communion Tent [on his own]. Why? He reasoned: My brother Aharon was anointed with the anointing oil, and he wears many priestly garments when performing the holy service, yet G-d said to me, *Speak to your brother Aharon, and let him not enter at all times the inner sanctuary [i.e., the Holy of Holies]* (*Vayikra* 16:2). I am not appointed for this [service], so surely I should keep away from the Communion Tent. He stayed away from the Tent, and G-d agreed with his decision.

MOSHE BREAKS THE TABLETS

[We learned above:] Moshe broke the tablets [on his own]. Why?
The Rabbis said: Moshe went up to Heaven to receive the tablets
which were written and set aside since the six days of Creation, as
it says, *The tablets were made by G-d and written with G-d's script
engraved* [charus] *on the tablets* (*Shemos* 32:16). [The Hebrew
word for engraved has the same letters as the word free (cheirus).
Our sages teach us:] Do not read it as *charus* [engraved] but rather
as *cheirus* [freedom], for whoever learns Torah is a free man.

At that time, [when Moshe came up to Heaven to receive the
Torah] the ministering angels, [wishing to keep the Torah in
Heaven,] plotted against Moshe, appealing to G-d, "Master of the
universe, *What is frail man that You should remember him, and the
son of mortal man that You should be mindful of him? Yet, you have
made him but slightly less than the angels, and crowned him with respect and dignity. You have given him dominion over Your handi-
work, You placed everything under his feet, sheep and cattle, all of
them, even the beasts of the field; the birds of the sky and the fish of the
sea*" (*Tehillim* 8:5-8). Grumbling about him, they said: "What is
this man born of woman doing among us?" As it says, *You ascend-
ed on high, You have taken captives, you have taken gifts* [accusing
Moshe of taking the Torah down to earth] (*Tehillim* 68:19).

Carrying the tablets, Moshe joyfully went down the mountain.
But when he saw the misdeed they committed in making the gold-
en calf, he said to himself: "How can I give them the tablets? I will
be obligating them to observe major mitzvos and condemning
them to death at the hands of Heaven, for it says in the
Commandments, *Do not have any other gods before Me* (*Shemos*
20:3)." He turned back, but the seventy Elders, seeing him go
back, ran after him. He held on to one end of the tablets, and [at-
tempting to prevent him from returning them] the Elders took
hold of the other end of the tablets, as it says, *I grasped the two
tablets* (*Devarim* 9:17). The word "grasped" implies that someone
was trying to tear them away from him. But Moshe was stronger,

as it says, *And by all the strong hand and awesome power that Moshe displayed before the eyes of all Yisrael* (*Devarim* 34:12).

A PARABLE

R. Yose Hagelili says: Let me offer a parable. Compare this to a king who told his envoy: "Betroth to me a beautiful, gracious and decent girl." The envoy betrothed a girl [with these qualities], but afterwards discovered that she had been behaving promiscuously with another man. He immediately drew the following logical conclusion: "If I give her the *kesubah* (marriage contract) now, she will be liable to the death penalty. Rather, I will tear up the *kesubah*, and she will be free of my master peacefully."

So too, the righteous Moshe drew his own conclusion, saying: "How can I give these tablets to Yisrael? I will be obligating them to the most difficult commandments making them liable to the death penalty, for it is written on them *Whoever sacrifices to any deity other than G-d must be condemned to death* (*Shemos* 22:19). I had better break the tablets and make Yisrael mend their ways." And G-d agreed with him, for it says, [*the tablets*] *which [asher] you broke* (*Shemos* 34:1). [G-d said to Moshe:] Thank you for breaking them [the word *asher* is seen as cognate to *ishur*, approval. G-d approved it, and praised Moshe for breaking them.]

THE LETTERS FLEW UPWARD

Some say Moshe broke the tablets only after seeing the letters fly upward [to heaven], for it says, *I saw [an extraordinary sight] and behold you had sinned to Hashem your G-d* (*Devarim* 9:16). Seeing the letters fly upward, Moshe said to himself: How can I give blank tablets to B'nei Yisrael! Let me, rather shatter them, as it says, *I grasped the two tablets, and threw them down from my two hands, breaking them before your eyes* (*Devarim* 917). [He threw them down in full view of the people] so they would not say: "Where are the tablets that you brought down? The whole thing is a sham!"

Others say: Moshe broke the tablets only because he was told to do so by G-d, for it says, [at the end of a passage referring to replacing the tablets that Moshe broke], *and they remained there as Hashem had commanded me* (*Devarim* 10:5). *He commanded me*, means he was commanded to break them.

R. Eliezer b. Azariah says: Moshe broke the tablets only because G-d told him to do so, for it says, *All the signs and wonders and the strong hand and awesome power that Hashem sent him to perform . . . that Moshe displayed before the eyes of all Yisrael* (*Devarim* 34:11,12). Just as he performed [the wonders and miracles] on G-d's command, so too, [when he broke the tablets] with his strong hand, he acted on G-d's command.

KING CHIZKIAH TAKES THE INITIATIVE

4. King Chizkiah acted on his own in four instances, and G-d approved of his judgment.

(1) He hid the Book of Cures, [so that people should pray to G-d, rather than rely on the cures written in the book]. G-d approved, as it says, [King Chizkiah said:] *"I have done what is good in Your eyes"* (*Yeshayah* 38:3), the good he referred to, was hiding the Book of Cures.

(2) He crushed the copper serpent. G-d approved of his action, as it says, *He ground up the copper serpent that Moshe had made, for until those days the Children of Israel used to burn incense before it* (2 *Melachim* 18:4).

(3) He removed the high places and altars [which people had erected to serve Hashem outside of the Beis Hamikdash], and G-d approved of his action, as it says, *But is not Chizkiah the one who removed [the] high places and altars, telling the people of Yehudah and Yerushalayim, "You must prostrate yourselves before only one altar and burn offerings on it"* [i.e., the altar in the Beis Hamikdash] (2 *Divrei Hayamim* 32:12).

(4) He stopped up the waters of Gichon. G-d approved of his action, as it says, *He, Chizkiah, stopped up the upper source of the waters of Gichon, diverting them underground westward to the City of David. Chizkiah was successful in all his endeavors* (*Divrei Hayamim* 32:30).[26]

IYOV'S FENCE

5. What fence did Iyov make for his words? It says, *[He is] a perfect and upright man who fears G-d and shuns evil* (*Iyov* 1:8). "*He shuns evil*" teaches that Iyov stayed away from things leading to transgression; from things that are loathsome, and from things that merely seem loathsome. Why does the verse mention that he was *a perfect and upright man*? To indicate that Iyov was born circumcised.[27]

MEN WHO WERE BORN CIRCUMCISED

Adam, too, was born circumcised, for it says, *G-d created man in His image*, [and G-d is perfect] (*Bereishis* 1:27).

Shes, [Adam's son], was also born circumcised, for it says, *[Adam] had a son in his likeness* (*Bereishis* 5:3).

Noach, was born circumcised, for it says, *Noach was a righteous man, perfect* [tamim] *in his generation* (*Bereishis* 6:9), [and *tamim* alludes to *milah*].

Shem, was born circumcised, for it says, *Malkitzedek king of Shalem* (*Bereishis* 14:18). [Malkitzedek was another name for Shem, and *shalem* means "perfect".]

---

[26] The Gichon Spring was east of Yerushalayim. Chizkiah dug a long tunnel diverting the water westward into the city itself, so that the Assyrians would not have access to it.

[27] The word *tam* "perfect" alludes to circumcision, as in the case of Avraham's circumcision where it says, *Walk before Me and be perfect* [tamim] (*Bereishis* 17:1) (*Ben Avraham*).

Yaakov, was born circumcised, for it says, *Yaakov was a perfect* [tam] *man who remained within the tents* (*Bereishis* 25:27).

Yosef, was born circumcised, for it says, *These are the offspring of Yaakov, Yosef...* (*Bereishis* 37:2). By rights it should say, "These are the offspring of Yaakov, Reuven" [for Reuven was Yaakov's oldest son]. Why does it say *Yosef*? To teach us that just as Yaakov was born circumcised, so too, Yosef was born circumcised.

Moshe, was born circumcised, for it says, *She saw that he was good* (*Shemos* 2:2). What did his mother see in him that made him more beautiful and delightful than other babies? She saw that he was born circumcised.

The wicked Bilam, was born circumcised, for it says, *The words of the one who hears the saying of G-d* (*Bamidbar* 24:4)[28]

Shmuel, was born circumcised, for it says, *The boy Shmuel kept growing and improving* (vetov) (1 *Shmuel* 2:26).[29]

David, was born circumcised, for it says, *A song of the michtam.*[30] *Protect me O G-d, for I have sought refuge in You* (*Tehillim* 16:1).

Yirmeyah, was born circumcised, for it says, *Before I formed you in the belly I knew you, and before you left the womb I established you as a prophet unto the nations* (*Yirmeyah* 1:5).

Zerubavel, was born circumcised, for it says, *I will take you, Zerubavel son of Shealtiel, My servant—the word of Hashem—and I will make you like [My] seal* (*Chaggai* 2:23).[31]

IYOV'S STRICT MORALITY

[Having digressed, the Mishnah now returns to the description of the fence Iyov made for his words.]

---

[28] Surely if G-d spoke to him he was circumcised; he was must have been born circumcised because it does not say anywhere that he underwent *milah* (*Ben Avraham*).

[29] *Tov* alludes to *milah*, as in the case of Moshe (*Shemos* 2:2).

[30] A musical instrument. The word *michtam* is seen as a contraction of *makaso tammah*, "His wound was whole," meaning, the place of the wound of *milah* was whole, because he was born circumcised (*Sotah* 10b).

[31] *Milah* is G-d's "seal of the covenant."

[Iyov said,] *I forged a covenant for my eyes not to gaze on a maiden* (*Iyov* 31:1). Iyov was stringent with himself, not even looking at an unmarried girl. A logical conclusion can be drawn: If Iyov did not look at a girl whom he could marry, or could marry off to his son, brother, or a relative, surely he did not look at another man's wife! Why was Iyov so strict with himself, never looking at a girl? He said: If I look at her today, and tomorrow another man marries her, I will end up having immoral thoughts about a married woman.

THE FENCE OF THE PROPHETS

6. What was the fence the prophets made for their words? It says, *Hashem will go forth like a mighty warrior, He will arouse vengeance like a man of war. He will shout triumphantly, even roar* (*Yeshayah* 42:13). G-d is not just like one mighty warrior, He is like all the mighty warriors in the world. [The prophets described G-d with metaphors, as a fence, to enable us to relate to Hashem who is beyond description]

Similarly, [the prophet says,] *The lion has roared, who will not fear? Hashem, G-d has spoken, who will not but prophesy?* (*Amos* 3:8). G-d is not just like one lion, but like all the lions in the world, [however the prophet describes Him in a way people can understand].

The same way, *And behold, the glory of the G-d of Yisrael was coming from the east. Its sound was like the sound of a multitude of waters, and the earth shone with His glory* (*Yechezkel* 43:2).

The sound of a multitude of waters refers to the angel Gavriel.

and the earth shone with His glory refers to the presence of the *Shechinah*. [The prophet is using similes as a fence while portraying lofty spiritual concepts.]

We can draw a logical conclusion from this: If Gavriel, who is only one of an infinite number of angels standing before G-d, has a voice that resounds to the ends of the world, how much more so, G-d, the King of kings who created the entire universe and all the higher and lower beings! [Therefore, how can we compare Him to earthly creatures?] But the prophets [made a fence for their words] using figurative language to convey esoteric concepts.

THE FENCE OF THE WRITINGS

7. What is the fence the Writings made for their words? It says, *Keep yourself far away from her; do not come near the doorway of her house* (*Mishlei* 5:8).

Keep yourself far away from her refers to heretics. When a man is told: "Don't mingle with heretics and don't visit their dens, for you will be led astray by them," he might answer: "I am sure of myself. Even if I associate with them, I will not go wrong." Or [he might answer]: "I will listen to their arguments, but I will not be swayed by them." Therefore, the verse says, *All who come to her do not return, nor do they attain the paths of life* (*Mishlei* 2:19). [The warning to keep away from non-believers for fear they will lead you astray, is the fence.]

[Another example of a "fence" in the Writings is:] It says, *She prepared her meat, mixed her wine and also set her table* (*Mishlei* 9:2). This passage also alludes to heretics. When a man enters their circle, they feed him, give him drink, clothe him, offer him shelter, and give him a lot of money. As soon as he becomes a member, they take it all away from him. It says about them, *Until the arrow splits his liver, he is like a bird hurrying to the trap, unaware that his life will be lost* (*Mishlei* 7:23).

Another interpretation [of the above mentioned verse (5:8):] *Keep yourself away from her* refers to a prostitute. A man is warned: "Don't walk in this street, and don't enter this alley, for a good-looking and charming prostitute lives there." When he says, "I am sure of myself. Even if I go there, I will not be led astray by her," he is told: "Although you are sure of yourself, don't enter there, for you may go wrong," as it says, *She has felled many victims; the number of her slain is huge* (*Mishlei* 7:26). [The Writings use metaphors as a fence to keep a man from transgressing.]

THE FENCE OF THE SAGES

8. What fence did the Sages make for their words? They said: You are allowed to recite the evening *Shema* [only] until midnight. R. Gamliel said: Until the rooster crows. How is this a fence? It prevents a man, returning home after a full day's work in the field, from saying: "I'll go home, eat a little, drink a little, take a nap, and then recite the *Shema*, [for I have all night to do it]." Meanwhile he will sleep the whole night. Instead, when a man returns home in the evening, he should go to the synagogue or *beis midrash* and read the Torah, if he is used to that, or study the Mishnah, if he is used to that, and then recite the *Shema* and *Shemoneh esrei* [before midnight]. Whoever transgresses the words of the Sages deserves to die.

R. Shimon b. Gamliel says: Sometimes a man may recite the *Shema* twice in one night, once immediately before the dawn rises, and once immediately after the dawn rises, thereby fulfilling his obligation for the day and for the night. [Hearing this,] the Sages made a fence for their words [ruling that you are allowed to recite the evening *Shema* only until midnight.]

9. [Another example of a "fence" by the Sages is found in the first Mishnah in *Avos*, where it says:] "Develop many disciples." The School of Shammai says: One should teach only a student who is smart, humble, of reputable ancestry, and wealthy,[32] but the School of Hillel says: One should teach everyone,[33] for there were many sinners who were drawn to learning Torah, and from them came forth righteous, pious, and respectable Jews.

---

[32] so that he should be able to learn without having to worry about his daily bread (*Binyan Yehoshua*).

[33] The "fence" of *Beis Hillel* is: The rebbi should teach the mystical aspects of the Torah only to a student who is worthy of it, while teaching the plain meaning to everyone according to his ability (*Binyan Yehoshua*)

CHAPTER THREE

SAYINGS OF RABBI AKIVA

1. R. Akiva says: Whoever takes a *perutah* (small coin) from charity when he does not need it, will not pass from this world before actually needing charity.

He used to say: A man who ties a rag around his eyes or waist, [fraudulently] crying: "Help the blind! Help the sick!" will end up suffering from this condition.

He used to say: He who steps on bread or throws money in a fit of anger, will not pass from the world before he approaches people for a handout.

2. He used to say: A person who tears his clothes, or breaks his vessels in anger, will end up worshipping idols. For such is the cunning strategy of the evil impulse: Today it will tell a person: "Tear your clothes!," and tomorrow it will tell him: "Worship idols!," and he will worship them.

3. He used to say: Whoever eyes his wife, hoping she will die so he may take her inheritance, or marry her sister, and whoever eyes his brother, hoping he will die so he may marry his wife, will be buried in their lifetime. The verse has him in mind when it says, *He who digs a pit will fall into it, and he who breaks down a wall will be bitten by a snake* (*Koheles* 10:8).

THE CASE OF THE WRONGED WOMAN

4. Once, a man uncovered a woman's head in the street. When she complained to R. Akiva he ordered the offender to pay

her four hundred *zuz*. Said the man: "Rabbi, allow me time [to pay the judgment]." R. Akiva agreed.

Arriving home, his friend told him: "With my advice, you will not have to pay her even one penny."

"Please advise me," he replied.

"Buy an *issur*'s worth of oil," said the friend [who knew the woman was very poor], "and break the bottle in front of the woman's door." [He did exactly that.]

What did the woman do? She came out of the house [and, seeing the spilled oil,] uncovered her hair, dipped her hand in the oil, and daubed her head with it.

The man had stationed witnesses to observe her. He then said to R. Akiva: "To this shameless woman I should pay 400 *zuz*? Why, for an *issur*'s worth of oil she did not mind bringing shame on herself! She went outside and uncovered her head, daubing it with oil!"

"Your argument does not hold water," R. Akiva retorted, "for although a person is not permitted to injure himself, he is not liable when he does, however if someone else injures him he is liable. So too, although she abused herself, she is not liable; but you who abused her, must give her the 400 *zuz*!"

SOW YOUR SEED IN THE MORNING

5. R. Dustai b. R. Yannai says: If you cultivated your field[34] and sowed in the first rainfall, sow again in the second rainfall. For if a hailstorm ruins the first planting, the second will survive. As it says, *Sow your seed in the morning, and don't hold back your hand in the evening, since you don't know which is going to succeed, the one or the other, or if both are equally good* (*Koheles* 11:6).

If you tilled the soil and sowed during the first and second rainfall, sow again during the third rainfall, for if a storm strikes the world and the first sowings are destroyed, the last will survive, *since*

---

[34] translation according to *Binyan Yehoshua*.

*you don't know which is going to succeed, the one or the other, or if both
are equally good. So sow your seed in the morning.*

LEARN TORAH NO MATTER WHAT

6. R. Yishmael says: If you learned Torah when you were
young, don't say, "I will not learn in my old age." Instead,
learn Torah [at all times], *for you don't know which* [learning] *is
going to succeed.* If you learned Torah when you were rich, do not
sit idle in poverty. If you learned Torah with a full stomach, do not
sit idle when you are hungry. If you learned Torah in comfort, do
not sit still under pressure. For one thing [achieved] in distress is
better than a hundred in comfort,[35] as it says, *Sow your seed in the
morning, and don't hold back your hand in the evening*[36].

R. Akiva says: If you studied Torah in your youth, study Torah
in your old age. Don't say: "I will not study Torah in my old age,"
for you don't know which [learning] *is going to succeed, the one or the
other, or if both are equally good.*

R. Meir says: If you learned from one teacher, don't say: "That's
enough for me." Instead, go to a teacher [who is more astute than
the first one[37]] and learn Torah from him. Don't go to a teacher
[who lives far away], but go to one who lives near you [to save the
travel expenses[38]], as it says, *Drink water* [i.e., learn Torah] *from
your own cistern and flowing water from your own well* [i.e., from
the teacher who lives in your town] (*Mishlei* 5:15).

A man is obligated to attend to three Torah scholars, such as R.
Eliezer, R. Yehoshua, and R. Akiva, for it says, *Praiseworthy is the
person who listens to me, to hasten to my doors* [dalsosai] *every day, to
the doorposts of my entranceways* (*Mishlei* 8:34). Do not read *dalso-*

---

[35] The reward is in proportion to the effort (*Avos* 5:26).

[36] Meaning if you learned in the morning when it was easy, continue to learn even
when things get difficult.

[37] *Ben Avraham.*

[38] *Ben Avraham.*

sai (*my doors*); read instead, *deles dalsosai*,[39] *for you don't know which* [learning] *is going to succeed, the one or the other, or if both are equally good*, as it says, *Sow your seed in the morning*.

GETTING MARRIED

R. Yehoshua says: Marry when you are young, and marry in your old age. Father children when you are young, and father children in your old age. Don't say: "I will not marry in my old age." On the contrary, marry and have sons and daughters, bringing more children into the world. *For you don't know which are going to succeed, the one or the other, or if both are equally good*, as it says, *Sow your seed in the morning, and don't hold back your hand in the evening*.

7. He used to say: If you gave a *perutah* to a poor man in the morning, and another poor man comes in the evening, give him too; for you do not know which will succeed, the one or the other, or if both are equally worthy, as it says, *Sow your seed in the morning*.

THE DEAD HAVE KNOWLEDGE OF THE WORLD

8. A pious man gave a *dinar* to a poor man on the eve of Rosh Hashanah in a year of famine. When his wife took him to task for it, he spent the night in the cemetery. There he heard the spirits [of two dead girls] talking to each other.

Said one to the other: "My dear, let's roam around the world, and hear from behind the curtain [that separates this world from the Divine Presence] what punishment is coming to the world [in the divine judgment decreed on Rosh Hashanah]."

---

[39] *deles* "one door" and *dalsosai* "two doors" adds up to three doors, alluding to the three Torah scholars one should serve.

Said her companion: "I can't go, because I am buried in a mat of reeds [instead of in linen shrouds]. You go, and whatever you hear, you'll tell me."

The first one went, wandered around, and returned. Said her companion: "My dear, what have you heard from behind the curtain?"

She replied: "I heard that anyone who plants after the first rainfall will find his crops destroyed by hail."[40]

[Overhearing this] the man did not plant until the second rainfall. As a result, everyone's crop was destroyed, but his survived.

The next year he spent the night in the cemetery again and heard the two spirits talking to each other. Said one to the other: "Let's roam around the world, and hear from behind the curtain what punishment is coming to the world."

Replied the other: "My dear, didn't I tell you that I am unable to go because I am buried in a mat of reeds? You go, and whatever you hear, come and tell me."

The first one went, roamed around the world, and returned. "My dear, what have you heard from behind the curtain?" her companion asked her. She replied: "I heard that anyone who plants after the second rainfall will have his crops struck with blight, [which destroys the tender shoots but does not harm the stronger stalks]."

The man planted after the first rainfall, with the result that everyone else's crop was blighted and his was not.

His wife asked: "Why was everyone else's crop damaged last year besides yours, and this year everyone else's crop is blighted yet yours is not?" He told her the whole story.

Shortly afterward, the wife of that pious man got into an argument with the mother of one of the girls [whose spirits the pious

---

40 In Eretz Yisrael there are three periods of rainfall. Crops that were planted during the first period, which begins on 17 Marcheshvan, will have grown rigid stalks by the second period and will be broken by the hailstorm that will occur at that time. However, the crops that were planted during the second period will still be very tender and will bend in the hailstorm and not be ruined by it (*Rashi* on *Berachos* 18b).

man had overheard talking]. Said the wife to the girl's mother: "Your daughter is buried in a mat of reeds!"

The next year the pious man again spent the night of Rosh Hashanah in the cemetery, and heard the two spirits talking to each other. Said one to the other: "Come let's roam around the world and hear from behind the curtain what punishment is coming on the world." Said the other: "My dear, leave me alone. The things we discussed have already been overheard by the living."

TZEDAKAH SAVED HIS LIFE

9. A pious man regularly gave charity. Once, he set sail on a ship, and a raging storm sank the ship in the middle of the sea. R. Akiva [sailing on another ship] saw the ship sink and came before the *beis din* to testify that the man's wife could remarry. Before he could take the stand, the man came and stood before him.

"Aren't you the one who drowned at sea?" Rabbi Akiva asked.

"Yes," he replied.

"Who raised you up from the sea?"

"The *tzedakah* I gave raised me out of the sea," he replied.

"How do you know this?" R. Akiva asked.

"When I sank to the depths of the sea, I heard a loud noise of the waves talking to each other. "Hurry, let's raise this man out of the sea, for he gave charity all his life!" they said.

Hearing this, R. Akiva raised his voice, declaring, "Blessed be G-d, the G-d of Yisrael, who has chosen the words of the Torah and the words of the Sages, which endure forever, as it says, *Send your bread upon the waters, for after many days you will find it* (*Koheles* 11:1), and it says, *Charity rescues from death* (*Mishlei* 10:2).

10. A woman approached Binyamin the *Tzaddik*, the secretary of the communal charity fund. "Rabbi, give me money to buy food," she cried.

"I swear, the charity fund is empty!," he replied.

"Rabbi," she said, "if you don't take care of me, you will be responsible for the death of a widow and her seven sons."

He gave her money from his own pocket.

Later, Binyamin the *Tzaddik* became sick and lay in bed with pain. Said the ministering angels to the Holy One, blessed be He, "Master of the universe, You said, 'Whoever saves a single soul in Yisrael is as though he had saved a whole world.' How much more so Binyamin the *Tzaddik* who saved a widow and her seven sons! Yet he is in bed suffering excruciating pain."

Immediately, his death sentence was torn up, and twenty-two years were added to his life.

CHAPTER FOUR

THE THREE PILLARS OF THE WORLD

1. **Shimon Hatzaddik was among the survivors of the Great Assembly.[41] He used to say: The world depends on three things—on Torah study, on the worship [of G-d], and on kind deeds (Avos 1:2).**

THE SUPREMACY OF TORAH STUDY

How do we know the world depends on Torah study? It says, *For I desire kindness, not sacrifice; and knowledge of G-d more than burnt-offerings* (*Hoshea* 6:6). A burnt-offering is the most cherished of all sacrifices, for the burnt-offering is entirely consumed by

---

[41] The Great Assembly was a group of 120 Sages who led the Jewish people at the beginning of the Second Beis Hamikdash era. It included the last prophets, including Ezra, Mordechai, Chaggai, Zechariah, and Malachi.

flames, as it says, *The priest shall burn the entire [animal] on the altar* (*Vayikra* 1:9), and elsewhere it says, *Shmuel took a suckling lamb and offered it up entirely as a burnt-offering to Hashem* (1 *Shmuel* 7:9). Yet the study of Torah is more beloved by G-d than burnt-offerings. For if a man learns Torah he will know the will of G-d, as it says, *Then you will understand the fear of Hashem, and discover the knowledge of G-d* (*Mishlei* 2:5). From here we learn that when a sage expounds to a congregation, Scripture considers it as if he offered fat and blood on the altar.

If two Torah scholars are learning Torah, and a bridal or funeral procession passes outside, they should not interrupt their study if there are enough people in the procession, but they should rise and gladden the bride or escort the dead if there are not enough people in the procession.

2. Once, as R. Yehudah b. Ila'i was teaching his students, a bridal party passed. He took a myrtle twig and danced, [waving] it before the bride until she passed out of sight.

3. Another time as R. Yehudah b. Ila'i was teaching his students a bridal party passed by. "What is that?" he asked.

"A bride is passing by," they replied.

"My sons," he said, "go out and gladden the bride. For we find that the Holy One, blessed be He, concerned Himself with a bride, how much more so should we!"

Where does it say that the Holy One, blessed be He, concerned Himself with a bride? In the verse, *G-d built* (vayiven) *the rib* (*Bereishis* 2:22). In the coastal towns, braiding is called *binaita* [related to the word *vayiven*]. This tells us that the Holy One, blessed be He, braided Chavah's hair, adorned her like a bride, and brought her to Adam, as it says, *He brought her to the man* (*Bereishis* 2:22). At the first [wedding], G-d acted as best man for Adam; ever since then a man must get his own best man.

It says, *[Adam said,] "Now this is bone from my bone and flesh from my flesh"* (*Bereishis* 2:23). At the first [wedding], Chavah was taken from Adam himself; ever since then a man marries a daughter of his friend.

AVODAH, SERVICE OF G-D

4. How do we know [the world depends] on the service of G-d? As long as the service in the Beis Hamikdash is ongoing, the world is blessed, and the rains come down in season, as it says, *If you love Hashem your G-d, serving Him with all your heart and soul, [then G-d promises]: "I will grant the fall and the spring rains in your land at the proper time . . . I will grant forage in your fields for your animals* (*Devarim* 11:13-15). But when the service in the Beis Hamikdash is not performed, the world is not blessed, and the rains do not come down in season, as it says, *Be careful that your heart is not tempted to go astray . . . He will lock up the skies so that there will not be any rain* (*Devarim* 11:16,17).

Furthermore it says, *And now take thought from this day and previously, before stone was placed upon stone in the House of Hashem, when they would come to a grain heap [of what would have been] twenty [units] but was [only] ten; [when one would come] to the winepress to draw out fifty [units] from the pit, but there were [only] twenty* (*Chaggai* 2:15,16).

Why does it not say about the winepress *"instead of twenty units there were only ten"* as it says about the grain? Because the yield of the winepress is a better indication of the year's prosperity than the wheat crop.[42] This teaches us that when the wine production dwindles it is a bad sign for the rest of the year.

Said Yisrael to the Holy One, blessed be He, "Master of the universe, why did You do this to us?"

G-d answered, *"You looked for much [produce], but, behold, it is little . . . because My House is ruined, while you run, each to his own*

---

[42] When there is an abundance of wine, people are optimistic and overestimate the yield (*Ben Avraham*).

house" (*Chaggai* 1:9). But if you involve yourself in the service of the Beis Hamikdash, I will bless you as in the beginning, as it says, *Take note . . . from the twenty-fourth day of the ninth month, from the day that the foundation was laid for Hashem's Sanctuary . . . while the seed is yet in the granary, and the vine, fig tree, pomegranate, and olive tree have not yet borne fruit. From this day on I will send blessing* (*Chaggai* 2:18,19).

From this we learn that the Holy One, blessed be He, cherishes the service of the Beis Hamikdash more than any other service.

KIND DEEDS

5. How do we know that [the world depends] on kind deeds? From the verse, *For I desire kindness, not sacrifice* (*Hoshea* 6:6). In the beginning, the world was created only with kindness, as it says, *For I said, "The world is built with kindness; the heavens, You establish Your faithfulness in them"* (*Tehillim* 89:3).

Once, R. Yochanan b. Zakkai was leaving Yerushalayim and R. Yehoshua was walking behind him. Seeing the Beis Hamikdash in ruins, R. Yehoshua cried, "Woe is to us that this place where the sins of Yisrael were atoned is laid waste!"

"My son," R. Yochanan said soothingly, "don't feel bad. We have another atonement that is just as effective as this, namely, acts of kindness, for it says, *For I desire kindness, not sacrifice* (*Hoshea* 6:6)."

DANIEL'S KIND DEEDS

Similarly, we find that Daniel, that precious man, engaged in acts of kindness all his life. What were the acts of kindness that Daniel did? You cannot say he offered burnt offerings and sacrifices [to G-d] in Babylon, for it says, *Be careful not to offer burnt offerings in any place that you may see fit. It must be done in the place that*

*Hashem shall choose [in the territory of] one of your tribes. Only there
shall you sacrifice burnt offerings (Devarim 12:13,14).*

What then were the acts of kindness Daniel did? He provided for
a bride and rejoiced her heart, escorted the dead, gave a *perutah* to
a poor man, and prayed three times a day. And his prayer was received with favor, as it says, *When Daniel learned that [the decree]
had been put in writing, he went home. He had windows made in his
upper chamber facing Yerushalayim, and three times a day he knelt
down and prayed, giving thanks before his G-d, exactly as he used to
do before this (Daniel 6:11).*

RABBI YOCHANAN AND VESPASIAN[43]

When Vespasian [the Roman general] came to destroy
Yerushalayim, he said [to the people of Yerushalayim]: "Fools, why
are you trying to destroy this city and burn the Temple [by refus-
ing to surrender]? All I ask is that you send me one bow and arrow
[as a token of submission], and I will withdraw [my forces]."

[The *Biryonim*[44]] said to Vespasian: "Just as we fought against
the first two[45] who were here before you killing them, so will we
fight against and kill you."

When R. Yochanan b. Zakkai heard this he summoned the
[heads of the *Biryonim*] telling them; "My children, why do you
want to destroy our city and cause the Beis Hamikdash to be

---

[43] Since R. Yochanan b. Zakkai was mentioned above in connection with the destruction of the Beis Hamikdash, another episode about his role in these tragic
events is related here.

[44] At that time there was a civil war raging in Yerushalayim among three Jewish fac-
tions: moderates who were followers of the Rabbis; the corrupt and assimilated
Sadducees who were Roman sympathizers and opponents of the Rabbis and *halachah*, and the Zealots [*Kana'im*], extreme nationalists who advocated open war-
fare to overthrow Roman domination. The violently militant members of the Zealot
party were called *Biryonim*.

[45] A reference to Florus and Cestius Gallus who were defeated by the Zealots in an
earlier uprising.

burned? All [Vespasian] wants is one bow or arrow, and he'll withdraw his forces."

They replied: "Just as we fought against the first two, who were here before him, killing them, so will we fight against and kill him."

Vespasian had [Jewish collaborators] stationed inside the walls of Yerushalayim. They wrote down every word they overheard, attaching the message to an arrow and shooting the arrow over the wall [making it appear as if they were attacking the Romans]. Overhearing what R. Yochanan told the *Biryonim*, they informed the Romans that R. Yochanan b. Zakkai was a Roman sympathizer.

Day after day, R. Yochanan pleaded with the *Biryonim* [to submit to Vespasian's demand]; it was to no avail. He then sent for his disciples, R. Eliezer and R. Yehoshua.

"My sons," he said to them, "Take me out of here. Make a coffin for me to lie in."

R. Eliezer carried the head of the coffin and R. Yehoshua carried the foot. As the sun set they reached the gates of Yerushalayim.

"Who is this?" the [*Biryonim*] gatekeepers inquired.

"A dead man," they replied. "Don't you know that a corpse may not be left overnight in Yerushalayim?"

"If it's a dead man," the gatekeepers said, "go ahead."

They carried him to Vespasian. When they opened the coffin, R. Yochanan stood up before him.

"Are you Rabbi Yochanan b. Zakkai?" Vespasian inquired, "Ask me a favor, and I will grant it."

[Seeing that Yerushalayim was lost, R. Yochanan wanted to preserve the spiritual heritage of the Jewish people,] so he requested, "Give me the city of Yavneh where I will teach my disciples, establish a prayer house and perform all the commandments of the Torah. [At least the Torah will survive and continue to flourish]."[46]

"Go," replied Vespasian, "and do whatever you want to do."

---

[46] R. Yochanan b. Zakkai's request to set up a yeshivah in Yavneh was of crucial importance. It was the instrument through which G-d ensured the continued existence of the Jewish people during the long exile.

Said R. Yochanan, "With your permission, I will tell you something."

"Speak," Vespasian answered.

Said R. Yochanan: "You are about to become the emperor of Rome."

"How do you know that?" Vespasian asked.

R. Yochanan replied: "We have a tradition that the Temple will not fall into the hands of a commoner, but to a king, for it says, *Lebanon will fall by a mighty one (adir)*" (*Yeshayah* 10:34), [*adir* refers specifically to a king, and *Lebanon* refers to the Beis Hamikdash].

Three days later, messengers arrived from Rome reporting that the emperor had died, and that Vespasian had been elected as his successor.

A Roman ballista[47] was brought up against the wall of Yerushalayim. Boards of cedar were inserted into the ballista, and hurled against the wall until it was breached. Then they placed a swine's head in the ballista, hurling it toward the sacrifices on the altar.

R. Yochanan b. Zakkai fearfully awaited the report that Yerushalayim was conquered, just as Eli sat and waited [to hear what had happened to the Ark in the battle against the Philistines], as it says, *Eli was seated in a chair next to the road, looking out, for his heart was fearful about the Ark of G-d* (1 *Shmuel* 4:13). When R. Yochanan b. Zakkai heard that Yerushalayim was destroyed and the Beis Hamikdash burned, he and his disciples tore their clothes, crying and mourning tearfully.

It says, *Open your doors, O Lebanon, and let fire consume your cedars!* (*Zechariah* 11:1).

Open your doors, O Lebanon refers to the Beis Hamikdash.

And let fire consume your cedars refers to the kohanim in the Beis Hamikdash who threw their keys toward heaven, saying: "Master of the universe! Here are Your keys which You entrusted to us. Since we were not privileged to be faithful agents to do the King's work

---

[47] An engine used by the Romans for hurling missiles.

and to eat at the King's table, we herewith return the keys to you." Then the kohanim jumped from the roof and fell into the flames.

Avraham, Yitzchak, Yaakov, and the twelve tribes wept, crying mournfully, *Wail, O cypress, for the cedar has fallen, for the mighty ones have been vanquished; wail, O oaks of Bashan, because the impregnable forest has come down (Zechariah* 11:2).

Wail, O cypress for the cedar has fallen refers to the Beis Hamikdash.

For the mighty ones have been vanquished refers to Yisrael.

Wail, O oaks of Bashan refers to Moshe, Aharon, and Miriam.

Because the impregnable forest has come down refers to the Holy of Holies.

There is a sound of shepherds' wailing, for their power has been vanquished (Zechariah 11:3) refers to David and Shlomoh, his son.

There is a sound of young lions' roar, for the heights of the Jordan have been vanquished (Zechariah 11:3) refers to Eliyahu and Elisha.

DIFFERENCES AMONG MEN

6. A person is different than his neighbor in three ways: in voice, taste, and appearance.

G-d gave each person a different voice. Had He had not done so there would be a great deal of immorality in the world. A man would leave his house [at night], and another man would enter his home and take his wife. [For if all men had the same voice, she would not realize it was not her husband]. Therefore, G-d gave each person his own distinctive voice.

G-d gave each person a taste different from that of his neighbor. Had he not done so, people would envy each other [for everyone would hanker for the same thing]. Therefore G-d gave each person his own taste which differs from his neighbor's taste.

G-d made each person look different from anyone else. Had he not done so, women would not recognize their husbands, and men would not recognize their wives. Therefore, G-d made them look different.

CHAPTER FIVE

————— ◉ —————

REWARD IN THE HEREAFTER

1. Antigonus of Socho received the tradition from Shimon the Just. He used to say: Don't be like servants who serve their master for the sake of receiving a reward, instead be like servants who serve their master not for the sake of a reward, [but out of love], and let the awe of Heaven be upon you, so that your reward will be doubled in the World to Come[48] (Avos 1:3).

2. Antigonus of Socho had two disciples [Tzadok and Baysos] who distorted the meaning of their teacher's words. They taught [their falsified version] to their disciples, and their disciples to their disciples.[49] [The disciples] analyzed these [faulty teachings] and said: "Why did our teachers say [to serve G-d without expecting a reward]? Is it possible that a laborer should work all day and not get paid in the evening?" Had our teachers believed there is a hereafter and a resurrection of the dead, they would not have said this.

Therefore they turned their back on the Torah and split into two sects, known as *Tzadokim* (Sadducees) and *Baysosim* (Boethusians).[50] They used silver and gold vessels all their lives, saying arro-

---

[48] The last segment "so that your reward will be doubled in the World to Come" does not appear in *Avos* 1:3. Tzadok and Baysos obviously did not include it in their teaching.

[49] Translation and interpretation according to *Ben Avraham*.

[50] They denied both the truth of the Oral Tradition and the authority of the Sages to interpret the Torah and to issue decrees. They also said that there is neither reward nor punishment in the World to Come; indeed they denied its existence.

gantly[51], "The *Perushim* (Pharisees)[52] have a tradition to afflict themselves in this world; yet in the World to Come they will have nothing!"

CHAPTER SIX

―――≈《◎》≈―――

TEACHINGS OF YOSE B. YOEZER

1. Yose b. Yoezer says: Let your house be a meeting place for sages, sit in the dust of their feet, and thirstily drink in their words (Avos 1:4).

Let your house be a meeting place for sages. How should one fulfill this? A man's house should be open for the sages and their students and the students' students, [so that it becomes well known and] people say: I'll meet you at the place of so and so.

Another interpretation of: "Let your house be a meeting place for sages," is: When a Torah scholar asks you to teach him, teach him if you are able to do so, otherwise, let him go away immediately.

[A student] should not sit in your presence on a couch, a chair or a bench. Instead he should sit before you on the floor. He should take in every word you say with fear, awe, dread, and trembling.

2. **Sit in the dust of their feet.** How should one fulfill this? When a Torah scholar comes to the city, do not say, "I do

---

[51] Translation according to Gr"a.
[52]. The Rabbinic party, who upheld the Torah and mitzvos, believing in the Written and the Oral Torah.

not need him." Instead, go and listen to him, sitting on the floor, rather than on a couch, a chair or a bench. Take in every word he speaks with fear, awe, dread, and trembling just as our fathers received the Torah from Mount Sinai with fear, awe, dread, and trembling.

R. AKIVA'S BEGINNINGS

Another interpretation: "Sit in the dust of their feet," refers to R. Eliezer, and "thirstily drink in their words," refers to R. Akiva.

How did R. Akiva begin studying? He was forty years old and had never studied Torah. Once, standing by a well, [he saw a stone that had been hollowed out by the water eroding it over the years].

"Who hollowed out this stone?" he wondered.

"It is the water falling on it day after day," people told him. They asked "Don't you know that it says, *Stones are worn away by water* (*Iyov* 14:19)?"

R. Akiva thought to himself: "If the soft water can pierce this hard rock, surely the words of Torah which are as powerful as iron will be able to engrave themselves on my heart which is flesh and blood!" Immediately he turned to learning Torah.

R. Akiva and his son went together to a teacher of little children. "Rebbi, teach me Torah," R. Akiva said.

R. Akiva held up one end of the blackboard, and his son the other. The teacher wrote down *alef, beis* until *tav*, and he learned it. Then he taught him *sefer Vayikra*, and he learned it. He went on learning until he knew the whole Torah. Then he went to [the yeshivah of] R. Eliezer and R. Yehoshua. "My rabbis," he said to them, "explain the Mishnah to me."

When they told him one Mishnah, he secluded himself. He wondered: "Why is the *alef* shaped like this?[53] Why is the *beis* shaped like this? Why does it say this and that?" He returned and asked the Rabbis, but they could not answer.

---

[53] The letter *alef* is composed of two *yud*s separated by a *vav* (*Ben avraham*).

R. Shimon b. Elazar said: Let me compare this to a parable. A stonecutter hewed rocks in the mountains. One day he began chopping small chips with his pickax.

People asked him, "What are you doing?"

"I'm dislodging the mountain," he replied, "and I'll throw it into the Jordan River.

"You can't dislodge a whole mountain!" they told him.

But he kept chopping, until he hit upon a big rock. He crept under it, pried it loose, and hurled it into the Jordan, shouting, "You don't belong here; there is where you belong!"

That is what R. Akiva did with the teachings of R. Eliezer and R. Yehoshua.[54]

R. Tarfon said to him: "Akiva, Scripture has you in mind when it says, *From the waters of the deep He fashioned rivers; He brings secret things out into the light* (*Iyov* 28:11). Things concealed from men, R. Akiva brings to light."

Each day, R. Akiva gathered a bundle of straw; he sold part of it to provide for his food, and he used the other part for his other needs. His neighbors complained, "Akiva, you are ruining our health with the smoke [from burning straw]. Sell the straw to us, buy oil with the money, and learn by the light of an oil lamp."

"I use the straw for many purposes," he replied, "I learn by its light, I keep warm by its heat; and I sleep on it."

In the future, on Judgment Day, R. Akiva will cause all poor people to be found guilty. When they will be asked: "Why didn't you learn Torah?" If they reply, "Because we were poor," they will be told: "Wasn't R. Akiva more poor and forlorn?" If they answer, "Because of our children," they will be asked, "Didn't R. Akiva have many sons and daughters, and he supported them together with Rachel his wife"[55]

---

[54] He asked minor questions and was told "Why do you ask such insignificant things?" But in the end he derived many halachos from the tiny hook on the letter *yud* (*Ben Avraham*).

[55] *Ben Avraham* interprets these words as follows: "Because Rachel his wife had merit," he was able to learn, and therefore, the poor will not be found guilty on Judgment Day.

When R. Akiva was forty years old he began to learn Torah; thirteen years later he taught Torah to the multitudes. By the time he died, he owned tables of silver and gold, and climbed into his bed on golden ladders. His wife wore golden slippers and a golden ornament [with the city of Yerushalayim engraved on it].

His students said to him: "Rebbi, you put us to shame by what you have done for her [because we cannot give such gifts to our wives]."

He replied: "She suffered greatly for my sake, so I could learn Torah."[56]

RABBI ELIEZER BEN HYRKANUS' HUMBLE BEGINNINGS

3. How did R. Eliezer b. Hyrkanus begin learning Torah? Though he was twenty-two years old he had not yet learned any Torah. One day he said to himself; "I will learn Torah from R. Yochanan b. Zakkai. [Afraid it was too late for him to start learning,] his father Hyrkanus said: "You won't eat unless you plow the entire furrow."

He woke early in the morning, plowed the entire furrow [and then left for Yerushalayim]. It is said: That day was *erev Shabbos*, and he went for his Shabbos meal to his father-in-law. Some say: He did not eat anything from the sixth hour of *erev Shabbos* until six hours after *motza'ei Shabbos*.

Walking along the road he noticed a clump of earth [that looked like stone]. Some say it was cattle manure. He picked it up and put it in his mouth. He spent the night at a guest house.

When he appeared before Rabban Yochanan ben Zakkai in Yerushalayim, a bad breath emanated from his mouth. Said Rabban Yochanan ben Zakkai to him: "Eliezer, my son, have you eaten at all today?"

---

[56] See *Nedarim* 50a.

He did not answer.

Rabban Yochanan ben Zakkai asked him again, and again he did not answer.

Rabban Yochanan ben Zakkai summoned the owners of the guest house.

"Did Eliezer have anything to eat in your place?" he asked.

"We assumed he would be eating with you, Rabbi," they replied.

"And I assumed he was eating with you," he replied. "Between [my assumption] and your [assumption] we almost lost Rabbi Eliezer!"

Rabban Yochanan said to [Rabbi Eliezer]: "Just as bad breath rose from your mouth, so will your good name as a Torah scholar go forth."

When Hyrkanus heard that Rabbi Eliezer was learning Torah with Rabban Yochanan ben Zakkai, he decided: "I will go to Yerushalayim and disinherit my son Eliezer."[57]

It is said: That day Rabban Yochanan ben Zakkai sat expounding in Yerushalayim and all the great men of Yisrael sat before him. When he heard that Hyrkanus was coming, he appointed guards, telling them: "If Hyrkanus comes, do not let him sit down."

When Hyrkanus arrived they did not let him sit down. He made his way forward until he reached the place near Ben Tzitzis Hakeses, Nakdimon ben Gurion, and Ben Kalba Savua.[58] Trembling [with frustration because he could not disinherit his son in front of these great men], he sat down next to them.

It is told: On that day Rabban Yochanan ben Zakkai fixed his eyes on Rabbi Eliezer, saying:

"Give the lecture!"

"I can't," he replied.

---

[57] Since Rabbi Eliezer was already 22 years old and had not learned until now, his father did not believe he would be successful. His brothers also incited their father against him, saying: "He abandoned you in your old age, but after your death he will want an equal share in your inheritance!" (*Pirkei D'Rabbi Eliezer*)

[58] The three most prominent men in Yerushalayim.

Yet Rabbi Yochanan insisted he do so, and the disciples pushed him forward. Rising, he delivered a lecture about things no one had ever heard before. At each novel idea Rabban Yochanan ben Zakkai rose to his feet and kissed him on his head, exclaiming: "Rabbi Eliezer, you have taught me the truth!"

Before leaving, Hyrkanus, stood up and declared: "My Rabbis, I come to disinherit my son Eliezer. Now, all my possessions shall be given to Eliezer[59] and his brothers are herewith cut off without a cent."[60]

TZITZIS HAKESES AND NAKDIMON BEN GURION

Why was Tzitzis Hakeses called by that name? Because [keses means a couch, and] he reclined on a silver couch at the head of all the great men of Yisrael.

The daughter of Nakdimon ben Gurion, had a couch covered with a spread worth twelve thousand golden dinars; she spent a golden Tzuri dinar every Friday for Shabbos meals; and she was awaiting *yibbum*.[61]

Why was Nakdimon ben Gurion called by that name? Because the sun shone through (*nakedah*) for his sake [as will become clear from the following story.]

One year the Jews went up to Yerushalayim for the pilgrimage Yom Tov[62] and had no water to drink. Nakdimon asked a wealthy lord: "Lend me twelve wells of water until such-and-such date. If I do not return the twelve wells of water by the set date, I will give you [the enormous sum of] twelve *kikar* of silver."

---

[59] Not wanting to benefit from his Torah learning, Rabbi Eliezer did not accept this, saying: "I only want an equal share with my brothers." (*Pirkei D'Rabbi Eliezer*).

[60] Because they maligned him and provoked me against Eliezer.

[61] A childless widow must marry her late husband's brother in a *yibbum* marriage. If he declines to marry her, he must perform *chalitzah* (*Devarim* 25:5-10)

[62] Pesach, Shavuos, and Sukkos when all Yisrael had to appear in the Beis Hamikdash (*Devarim* 16:16).

When the loan was due, the lord sent him a message: "Give me either twelve wells of water or twelve *kikar* of silver."

Said Nakdimon: "I still have all day."

The lord mocked him, exclaiming, "All year long it has not rained, do you think it will rain now?"

He went happily to the bathhouse, and Nakdimon went to the beis midrash. Wrapping himself in his *tallis,* he prayed: "*Ribbono shel Olam*! You know full well that I did not do this for my glory, nor did I do it for the glory of my father's house; only for Your glory did I do this, so there should be water for the people going up to Yerushalayim for Yom Tov."

Immediately the sky turned dark with clouds and rain poured down, filing the twelve wells with water until they overflowed.

Nakdimon sent a message to the lord: "Send me the money for the excess water you received."

Replied the lord: "The sun has already set, and the water belongs to me [for it fell after the deadline, and you must pay me the twelve *kikar* of silver]."

Nakdimon went back to the beis midrash, wrapped himself in his *tallis* and prayed: "*Ribbono shel Olam*! Please perform another miracle for me, like the first one."

Immediately the wind blew and the clouds scattered, revealing the shining sun.

As he came out of the beis midrash he met the lord who said to him: "I know that the Holy One, blessed be He, made the world tremble only for your sake."[63]

KALBA SAVUA

Why was Kalba Savua called by that name? Because whoever entered his house hungry as a dog (*kelev, kalba*) left with a full stomach (*save'a, savua*— satiated).

---

[63] The hour of sunset had already passed, and only because of Nakdimon did G-d make the world shudder.

When the [Roman] Emperor Vespasian besieged Yerushalayim, the Zealots[64] tried to burn all the valuable property [of Kalba Savua]. Kalba Savua asked them: "Why are you destroying this city, by burning all these resources? Wait until I see what I have in the [storage] house.

He found he enough food to provide meals for every one in Yerushalayim for twenty-two years. He issued orders to pile up, sort, sift, knead and bake the food to provide for every person in Yerushalayim for twenty-two years. But the Zealots ignored him [and burned down all the supplies anyway.][65]

What did the [starving] men of Yerushalayim do? They brought loaves of dates, and bricked them into the walls, plastering them with clay [to hide them from the *Biryonim*.]

The men of Yerushalayim also boiled straw and ate it.

Men stationed on the walls of Yerushalayim would call out: "For five dates I will go down and bring back five [Roman] heads!" When he received five dates he would go down and chop off five heads from Vespasian's troops.

Seeing that their excrement contained no sign of grain, Vespasian said to his soldiers: "If these who eat nothing but straw kill so many of you, how much more would they kill, if they had everything you eat and drink!"

---

[64] These are the *Biryonim* described in *Gittin* 56b. Rashi explains ad.loc. these were worthless terrorists, who brought about the destruction of the Beis Hamikdash through their hatred and jealousy of each other.

[65] The *Biryonim* wanted to starve the people in order force them to confront the Romans in battle.

CHAPTER SEVEN

1.
Yose b. Yochanan, leader of Yerushalayim, says: Let your
house be open wide; treat the poor as members of your
household, and do not converse excessively with a woman
(Avos 1:5).

IYOV'S OPEN HOUSE

Let your house be opened wide. How should one fulfill this? A
man's house should have a wide entrance on the south, the east,
the west, and the north, like Iyov, who made four doors to his
house. Why did Iyov make four doors to his house? So the poor
would not have to take pains going all around the house; whether
one came from the north, south, east or west, he could enter di-
rectly.

Treat the poor as members of your household. This means to
treat the poor so they talk about what they ate in your house the
way the poor used to talk about what they had eaten and drunk in
Iyov's house. When [two poor men] met, one would ask the other:
   "Where are you coming from?"
   "From Iyov's house."
   "And where are you going?" the other would ask.
   "To Iyov's house," was the answer.
   When Iyov was stricken with the calamity [of severe boils], he
said to the Holy One, blessed be He: "Master of the universe, did
I not feed the hungry and give the thirsty to drink, as it says, *Did
I eat my food alone, the fatherless not eating of it also*? (*Iyov* 31:17).
And did I not clothe the naked, as it says, *Was there ever a destitute
person without clothing whose loins would not bless me, who would not*

warm himself by the shearings of my sheep? (*Iyov* 31:19,20).

The Holy One, blessed be He, said to Iyov: Iyov, you have not reached half of Avraham's measure. You sit in your house waiting for wayfarers to arrive. To one used to eating wheat bread, you serve wheat bread; to one used to eating meat you serve meat. To one used to drinking wine, you give wine to drink. But Avraham did not act like this. He went out looking for wayfarers and when he found them, he brought them into his house. He gave wheat bread to one who was not used to eating wheat bread; he served meat to one not used to eating meat; he gave wine to one not used to drinking wine. He also built large lodges on the highways, stocking them with food and drink, and every passing wayfarer ate, drank and blessed Heaven. That is why he was granted contentment,[66] as it says, *[Avraham] planted an,* "eshel" *in Beer-sheva* (*Bereishis* 21:33).[67]

HUMILITY

2.1 Teach the members of your household humility. If a poor man comes to the door of a humble man with a humble family, asking: "Is your father in?" they will answer, "Yes, please come in." Even before he steps inside, the table is set for him. When he eats, drinks and praises G-d, great happiness and contentment is bestowed on the master of the house.

But if a poor man stands at the door of one who is not humble and whose family members are quick-tempered, asking "Is your father in?" they will answer: "No," and scold him, angrily chasing him away.

Another interpretation: Teach the members of your household

---

66 He had a son at 100 years of age, and he did not suffer the calamities of Iyov (*Binyan Yehoshua*).

67 *Eishel* is seen as related to *sha'al* "to ask." He asked his guests, "Would you like to eat, grapes, figs or pomegranates?" *Midrash Rabbah* (*Binyan Yehoshua*).

humility. Why? If a humble man, whose family members are also humble, goes overseas, he will pray:

"I gratefully thank You, Hashem my G-d, that my wife does not quarrel with others." He is not afraid and his mind is at ease until he returns.

However if one is not humble and the members of his family are quick tempered, and he prays that his wife does not quarrel with others, his heart is fearful and his mind is not settled until he returns.

3. Do not engage in too much idle talk with women— even with your own wife, much less with your neighbor's wife. Anyone who engages in too much idle talk with women, brings trouble on himself, neglects Torah study, and will end up in Gehinnom.

Do not engage in too much idle talk with women. How should one fulfill this? If a man was not treated with respect in the house of study, or he had a fight with his neighbor, he should not go and tell his wife: "I had a fight with So-and-so, and this is what he said to me, and this is how I answered him." For in doing so he disgraces himself and disgraces his neighbor. His wife who used to treat him with respect, now ridicules him. When the neighbor [with whom he had the fight] hears of it, he cries: "Woe is me! He told his wife the things we quarrelled about!" The upshot is this person disgraces himself, disgraces his wife, and disgraces his neighbor.

CHAPTER EIGHT

1. Yehoshua b. Perachyah and Nitai of Arbel received the
   tradition from them.[68] Yehoshua b. Perachyah says:
Accept a teacher upon yourself; acquire a friend for yourself,
and judge everyone favorably (Avos 1:6).

LEARN WITH ONLY ONE TEACHER

Accept a teacher upon yourself. How should one fulfill this? Learn
[all subjects] from only one teacher, and study Scripture, Mishnah,
Midrash, Halachah, and Aggadah with him. If the teacher neglected to teach you something in Scripture, he will eventually teach it
to you when you learn Mishnah; if he neglected to tell you something when teaching you Mishnah, he will eventually teach it to you
when you learn Halachah; if he neglected to tell you something
when teaching you Halachah, he will eventually teach it to you
when you learn Aggadah. [By learning with only one teacher] you
stay in one place, and you are richly blessed with good fortune [i.e.,
you will become an accomplished Torah scholar].

2. R. Meir used to say: To whom can one compare a person
   who learns Torah with only one teacher? To a man who had
a single field, raising wheat on one part of it, barley on another part
of it, olive trees on a third part of it, and other trees on the last part
of it. That man is richly blessed with good fortune.

But one who learns with two or three teachers is like a man who
has many fields, raising wheat on one, barley on the second, olive
trees on the third and other trees on the fourth. That man must pay

---

68   From Yose b. Yoezer and Yosef b. Yochanan.

attention to many scattered fields, [leaving him] without good fortune and blessing.

STUDY PARTNERS

3. **Acquire a friend for yourself.** How should one do this? Acquire a study partner who will eat with you, drink with you, learn Scripture with you, learn Mishnah with you, share your room, and reveal the secrets of the Torah and refined social behavior to you.

When two [study partners] learn Torah together and one errs in a halachah or in a chapter heading, or says of something unclean that it is clean, or of something clean that it is unclean, or of a forbidden thing that it is permitted, or of a permitted thing that it is forbidden, his study partner will set him right. Where do we know that when his study partner corrects him and studies with him they are richly rewarded for their effort? It says, *Two are better than one, for they get a greater return for their labor* (*Koheles* 4:9).

4. When three people learn Torah together, the Holy One, blessed be He, considers it as one group dedicated to Him, as it says, *Who built His chambers in the Heavens and founded His group upon the earth; Who summons the waters of the sea and pours them over the land—Hashem is His name* (*Amos* 9:6). Thus, three who learn Torah together comprise one unified group before the Holy One, blessed be He.

5. When two are learning Torah together it is cherished on High, for it says, *Then those who fear Hashem spoke to one another, and Hashem listened and heard, and a book of remembrance was written before Him for those who fear Hashem and those who give thought to His Name* (*Malachi* 3:16).

[The phrase,] *Those who fear Hashem* refers to those [communal leaders] who issue a decree [to ransom captives, and are unafraid to

force the wealthy to pay the ransom money][69] saying: "Let us release the prisoners and ransom the captives!" The Holy One,
blessed be He, grants them success [in collecting the ransom], and
they act immediately.

[The phrase,] *Those who give thought to His Name* refers to those
[communal leaders who flatter the wealthy and are reluctant to im-
pose a levy on them,] saying [halfheartedly]: "Let's release the prisoners and ransom the captives." The Holy One, blessed be He,
does not help them [in collecting the ransom], and [in the mean-
time] an angel comes and strikes [the captives] down.[70]

6.
   When one learns Torah by himself, he is cherished on
High. For it says, *Let one sit in solitude and be silent, for He
has laid [his reward] upon him* (*Eichah* 3:28).

To what can this be compared? To a man who went to the market, leaving his little son alone at home. The child took down a
scroll [i.e., a book], placed it on his lap and [made believe he was]
studying. Returning from the market, the father exclaims: "Look
what my little son has done! I went to the market and left him
alone at home. He took down a scroll by himself, put it on his lap,
and is studying it!" Thus we learn that even when one sits by himself learning Torah, it is cherished on High.[71]

JUDGING EVERYONE FAVORABLY

7.
   Judge everyone favorably. A young girl was taken captive,
and two pious men tried to ransom her. One of them entered
a house of prostitution. When he came out he asked his partner:

---

[69] Translation according to *Ben Avraham*.

[70] Translation according to *Binyan Yehoshua*. According to *Ben Avraham*, the
angel strikes down the hesitant communal leaders.

[71] The analogy is: Even if the teacher or the study partner goes out, one should
continue learning by himself (*Ben Avraham*).

"What did you think of me?"

"[I thought you went in] to find out how much money they were demanding for her release," the other replied.

"I swear, that's exactly what happened!" the first answered, adding, "Just as you judged me favorably, so may the Holy One, blessed be He, judge you favorably."

8. Another time a young girl was taken captive and again two pious men tried to ransom her. One of them was arrested and charged with attempted abduction.[72] He was thrown in prison, and every day his wife brought him bread and water. One day he said to her: "Tell So-and-so [his colleague] that I am being held in prison because [I want to protect the girl[73] from] immorality, while he sits at home not caring what happens to the girl. [He should join me in prison and help me protect her.]"

Replied the wife: "Is it not enough that you are held in prison? You also want to dream up senseless schemes?"

"I implore you," he said to her, "please go." So she told [the colleague].

What did [the colleague] do? He brought silver and gold, and taking a group of men with him, they freed both [the pious man and the girl].

When he came out of prison the pious man said to them: "Let this girl sleep with me on a bed with her clothes on."[74]

In the morning he said to them: "Let me immerse in a *mikveh*."

They let him immerse, and they let her immerse.

Then he asked them: "When I asked to immerse, what did you think of me?"

---

[72] They suspected that he wanted to abduct the girl (*Ben Avraham*).

[73] He continued: "I really could escape from prison, but I am staying to protect the girl" (*Ben Avraham*).

[74] To demonstrate that this was the way he guarded her without ever stumbling into sin (*Ben Avraham*)

They replied: "We thought, you were hungry and thirsty in prison, and now that you were freed you regained your vigor, and perhaps had a discharge of semen.

"What did you suspect when the girl immersed?" he asked.

They replied: "We thought she ate and drank the heathens food when she was imprisoned, so you told her to immerse to become clean."

He said: "I swear! That is exactly what happened. Just as you judged me favorably, so may G-d judge you favorably."

THE ANIMALS OF THE RIGHTEOUS

Just as the *tzaddikim* of old were pious, so were their animals pious. The camels of Avraham our father would not enter a house in which there was an idol, as it says, [Lavan] said: *I myself have cleared out the house and a place for the camels* (*Bereishis* 24:31). [He said: *I have cleared out*—the idols—*from the house*. Why does it add, *And a place for the camels?*] To teach us that the camels would not enter Lavan the Aramean's property until he removed all the idols.

The donkey of R. Chaninah b. Dosa was stolen by robbers. They tied the donkey in a yard and placed straw, barley and water before it, but it did not want to eat or drink [because the food had not been tithed].

The robbers said: "Why should we let it die and smell up our yard?" They opened the gate and drove it out. It walked along until it reached R. Chanina b. Dosa's house. His son, hearing it bray said, "Father, this sounds like our animal." Said R. Chanina: "Son, open the door and let it in, for it is about to die from hunger." He opened the door, placed straw, barley, and water before it, and it ate and drank.

The Rabbis said: Just as the *tzaddikim* of old were pious, so were their animal pious [eating only food that was tithed].

CHAPTER NINE

1.
Nitai of Arbel said: Keep away from a bad neighbor; do not associate with a wicked person, and do not give up the belief in retribution (Avos 1:7).

WOE TO THE WICKED AND WOE TO HIS NEIGHBOR

Keep away from a bad neighbor:[75] Whether he is your neighbor indoors, outdoors, or in the field. For it says, *The iniquities of the wicked one will trap him* (*Mishlei* 5:22). This teaches us that plagues come only because of the sins of the wicked. The sins of the wicked cause the wall of the righteous to be torn down. How so? If a wall separates the wicked from the righteous, and a plague appears in the house of the wicked on the wall he shares with the righteous, the wall of the righteous has to be torn down[76] because of the sin of the wicked.

The Sages summed it up, saying: Woe to the wicked and woe to his neighbor! The sins of the wicked cause the wall of the righteous to be torn down.

TEN REBELLIOUS ACTS

2.
Our forefathers tested the Holy One, blessed be He ten times [through their lack of faith], but they were punished only for evil speech [which was one of the ten].

---

[75] I.e., one who spreads slanderous tales (*Ben Avraham*).
[76] *Vayikra* 14:34; *Nega'im* 12:6.

These are the trials: Twice at the Red Sea, [once when going down into the sea, and once when coming out]; once when the manna began to fall (Shemos 16:19), and once when the manna ceased to fall (Shemos 16:26); once when the first quail was seen (Shemos 16:3,13), and once when the last quail was seen (Bamidbar 11:4); once at Marah (Shemos 15:23 ff.), once at Refidim (Shemos 17:1 ff.), once at Chorev[77], and once when the spies returned (Bamidbar 13). The test of the spies was the gravest of them all, as it says, [in connection with the spies], *They tested me these ten times by not obeying Me (Bamidbar 14:22)*; and, *The men who had given a bad report about the land died before Hashem in the plague (Bamidbar 14:37)*.

We can draw a logical conclusion: If the Holy One, blessed be He, punished the spies for disparaging the land which has neither a mouth, nor a face, nor feeling of shame, how much more will the Holy One, blessed be He, punish one who insults, maligns and embarrasses his fellow [who does have a mouth, yet keeps quiet and does not respond in kind].

AHARON AND MIRIAM SPEAK AGAINST MOSHE

R. Shimon says: Those that spread slanderous tales will be stricken with plagues. It says about Aharon and Miriam that they slandered Moshe and were punished, as it says, *Miriam and Aharon began speaking against Moshe (Bamidbar 12:1)*.

Why does the verse mention Miriam before Aharon? This teaches us that Tzipporah told Miriam [that Moshe kept away from her];[78] Miriam told Aharon; then both of them spoke against that

---

77 When they made the golden calf, *Shemos* 32.

78 How did Miriam know that Moshe had separated himself from his wife? Rabbi Natan says: Miriam was standing next to Tzipporah when Moshe was told, "Eldad and Medad are prophesying in the camp" (v. 27). When Tzipporah heard this, she said: "I pity the wives of these men. If the husbands are required to prophesy they will separate themselves from their wives just as my husband separated himself from me" (*Rashi* on *Bamidbar* 12:1).

righteous man [Moshe]. For speaking against the righteous man, they received punishment, as it says, *Hashem displayed anger against them and He departed* (*Bamidbar* 12:9). Why does it say, *And He departed?* This teaches that Aharon was also stricken with leprosy, however it went away from Aharon and attached itself to Miriam, because Aharon did not engage in talebearing. But Miriam who did engage in talebearing was punished severely.

Miriam said: "I received a prophetic message, but I did not keep away from my husband." Aharon said: "I received a prophetic message, but I did not keep away from my wife. And our forefathers received prophetic messages, and they did not keep away from their wives. [Could it be that] Moshe, is keeping away from his wife out of arrogance?"

They did not pass judgment on him to his face, but in his absence. They did not denounce him with certainty, they only wondered whether Moshe [kept away from his wife] out of arrogance. We can draw a logical conclusion from this: If Miriam was punished for speaking against her brother, and she spoke without certainty, and did not speak to his face, how much greater will be the punishment of an ordinary person who insults and embarrasses his fellow to his face!

At that moment Aharon said to Moshe: "Moshe, my brother, do you think this leprosy affects only our sister Miriam? No! It affects our flesh too![79] This can be compared to a person holding a glowing coal in his hand. No matter how much he keeps juggling it, his flesh is still seared," as it says, *Let [Miriam] not be like a stillborn child, who comes from the womb with half its flesh rotted away*" (*Bamidbar* 12:13).

Thereupon Aharon appeased Moshe, saying: "Moshe, my brother, have we ever harmed anyone in the world?"

---

[79] [Text amended according to *Vilna Gaon.*] Aharon said to Moshe: "Since we are brothers and sister, the affliction of Miriam's flesh is tantamount to our own." It was as if Moshe and Aharon who were born from the same womb as Miriam, had half of their own flesh eaten away (Rashi on *Bamidbar* 12:12).

"No," he replied.

"If we never harmed anyone," said Aharon, "how could we possibly have wanted to harm you, our brother? But what can I do? We made an error. We overlooked the covenant between us, as it says, *They did not remember the covenant of brothers* (*Amos* 1:9). Now, for neglecting the covenant between us shall we lose our sister?"

Moshe drew a small circle, stood inside it, and pleaded for Miriam, saying: "I will not move away from here until Miriam my sister is healed." As it says, *Moshe cried out to Hashem, saying, "O G-d, please heal her!"* (*Bamidbar* 12:13).

The Holy One, blessed be He, replied: If a king had reproached her, if her father had reproached her, would she not be ashamed for seven days? How much more, when I, the King of kings rebuke her! By rights she should be ashamed for fourteen days. But for your sake, she shall be pardoned with seven days [of quarantine], as it says, *Hashem said to Moshe, "If her father had spit in her face . . ."* (*Bamidbar* 12:14).

MOSHE'S GREAT HUMILITY

[The Mishnah repudiates Aharon and Miriam's suspicion of Moshe being arrogant by quoting the verse,] *Moshe was very humble, more so than any man on the face of the earth* (*Bamidbar* 12:3).

[The Mishnah asks:] Perhaps he was humble because he was of puny stature? To tell you otherwise, it says, *[Moshe] spread the tent over the tabernacle* (*Shemos* 40:19). Just as the tabernacle measured ten cubits, so did Moshe measure ten cubits in height.

Was he more humble than the ministering angels? Impossible. For it says, *more so than any man*—but not more humble than the ministering angels.

Was he more humble than the early generations? Not so. For it says, *on the face of the earth*—more so than any man of his generation, but not more humble than the early generations.

[Reiterating Moshe's meekness, the Mishnah points out:] There are three kinds of skin disease: wet boils, dry boils, and polypus (a growth on the nose), [and people suffering from these disfiguring diseases are very humble]. But Moshe was more humble than the people afflicted with these diseases.

GEICHAZI'S AND UZZIAH'S PUNISHMENT

3. R. Shimon b. Elazar says: Plagues also strike people who tell lies, for we find that Geichazi, who told lies about his master [the prophet Elisha], suffered from leprosy until the day he died, as it says, [Elisha said to Geichazi,] *Naaman's leprosy shall therefore cling to you and to your children forever! When [Geichazi] left his presence, he was white as snow with leprosy* (2 *Melachim* 5:27).

He used to say: Plagues will strike the arrogant, for we find that this happened to Uzziah, as it says, *When he was strong, he grew so arrogant that he acted corruptly: he trespassed against Hashem his G-d by entering the Sanctuary of Hashem to burn incense on the incense altar. Azariah the Kohen and eighty other brave Kohanim of Hashem, confronted King Uzziah saying to him: "It is not for you, Uzziah, to burn incense to Hashem, but for the Kohanim, the descendants of Aharon who are consecrated to burn incense. Get out of the Sanctuary, for you have trespassed, there will be no glory in it for you from Hashem, G-d!" Uzziah, holding the censer ready to burn incense, became angry, but as he got angry with the Kohanim, leprosy broke out on his forehead in front of the Kohanim in the House of Hashem beside the incense altar* (2 *Divrei Hayamim* 26:16-19).

At that time the Sanctuary split into two parts, causing a gap twelve miles wide. *The Kohanim rushed him away from there, and he, too, hastened to leave, for Hashem had afflicted him. King Uzziah was a leper until the day of his death. He dwelt in his leprosy in a place of asylum, for he was banished from the Temple of Hashem. His son Yosam took charge of the royal house and judged the people of the land* (2 *Divrei Hayamim* 26:20,21).

4. **Do not associate with a wicked person.** One should associate neither with an evil man [i.e., a slanderer] nor a wicked

man. We find that Yehoshafat [king of Yehudah] associated with Achav [king of Yisrael] going up with him to Ramot-Gilad. G-d became furious with him, as it says, *Should you give aid to the wicked and befriend those who hate Hashem? Because of this, fury is upon you from Hashem* (2 *Divrei Hayamim* 19:2).

On another occasion [Yehoshafat] allied himself with Achaziah [king of Yisrael] building ships in Etzion-Gever [to create a fleet to go to Tarshish]. Hashem wrecked his undertakings, as it says, [The prophet said,] *"Because you have allied yourself with Achaziah, Hashem has wrecked your undertakings!" The ships broke down and they did not succeed in going to Tarshish* (2 *Divrei Hayamim* 20:37).

In the same vein, we find that Amnon associated with Yonadav, and Yonadav gave him evil advice, as it says, *Amnon had a friend named Yonadav, the son of David's brother Shim'ah, and Yonadav was a very cunning man* (2 *Shmuel* 13:3)—cunning in evil.

Another interpretation of "Do not associate with a wicked person," is: even as a study partner for learning Torah.

BELIEF IN DIVINE RETRIBUTION

5. **Do not give up the belief in retribution.** What does this mean? A man should always be fearful, thinking: "Woe is me! Perhaps disaster will strike me today, perhaps tomorrow."[80] As a result he lives in a constant state of anxiety. As it says about Iyov, *What I dreaded has come upon me* (*Iyov* 3:25).

6. Another interpretation of "Do not give up belief in retribution," is: When a man sees success he should not say: "Because I have merited it, G-d has given me food and drink in this world, and my reward remains intact in the World to Come." Instead he should say: "Woe is me! Perhaps G-d found that I did no more than one good deed, and He is rewarding me with food and drink in this world, so He may destroy me in the World to Come."

---

[80] The constant fear of calamity keeps him from transgressing (*Ben Avraham*).

CHAPTER TEN

—⇒◉⇐—

INSTRUCTIONS FOR JUDGES

1.   Yehudah b. Tabbai and Shimon b. Shetach received the tradition from them. Yehudah b. Tabbai says: [When serving as a judge] do not act as a lawyer; when litigants stand before you, consider them both as guilty; but when they leave, having accepted the judgment, consider them both as innocent (Avos 1:8).

2.   [When serving as a judge] do not act as a lawyer. How should one fulfill this? If you heard a case or a halachah in the study hall, do not rush to answer. Instead, calmly analyze why the question was raised, [and then render your decision fairly and objectively].

And when two litigants, one poor, the other rich, come before you, don't say: "How can I vindicate the poor and condemn the rich, [embarrassing him? I'll tell the poor man: 'You really are guilty; so pay him what you owe him.'"]

And don't say: "How can I vindicate the rich and condemn the poor? [After all, the rich is required to support the poor. I'll vindicate the poor; that way the rich will give him the money as charity]. Neither should you think: "If I condemn the poor man, he will hate me, and if I vindicate the poor man, the rich man will hate me. [What do I need this trouble for! I'll tell them to meet halfway.]"

And don't say: "How can I take the money from one and give it to the other?" [Remember,] the Torah says, *Do not give anyone special consideration when rendering judgment* (*Devarim* 1:17).

R. Meir used to say: What is implied by the verse, *Listen to the great and the small alike* (1:17)? The judge should not make one litigant stand while allowing the other to sit, nor allow one to speak all he wishes, while telling the other to be brief.

R. Yehudah says: I heard that if the judges wish to have both litigants sit, they may be seated. It is only forbidden for one to stand
while the other sits, and for one to speak all he wishes, while the
other is told to be brief.

Another interpretation of, *Listen to the great and the small:*
Consider a minor lawsuit, with the same seriousness as a major lawsuit; a lawsuit over a *perutah* like a lawsuit over a hundred *maneh.*

3. He [Yehudah b. Tabbai] used to say: Before I entered high
office, when someone would urge me: "Enter it," I would
wish to harass him to death. Now that I have attained high office,
when someone tells me to resign, I wish I could pour a kettle of
hot water on him. For just as it is hard to rise to high office, so is
it hard to be demoted from it. We find that this happened to Shaul.
When he was told: "Become the king!" he hid, as it says, *Hashem
replied, "Yes, he is hiding among the baggage"* (1 *Shmuel* 10:22), but
when he was told: "Give up [the throne]," he chased David and
wanted to kill him.

4. **Shimon b. Shetach says: Interrogate the witnesses thor-
oughly, because [they may be] deceivers, and be cautious with your words, lest they learn through them to falsify
(Avos 1:9).**

CHAPTER ELEVEN

LOVE WORK

1. **Shemayah and Avtalyon received the tradition from
them. Shemayah said: Love work, despise [positions of]**

leadership, and do not develop a close relationship with the government (Avos 1:10).

Love work: How is that to be understood? A man should love work and not hate [even a distasteful job]. Just as the Torah was given as a covenant, so was work given with a covenant, as it says, *Six days shall you work and accomplish all your work, and the seventh day is Shabbos to Hashem your G-d* (*Shemos* 20:9,10).[81]

R. Akiva says: There are times when a man works and thereby escapes death, and there are times when a man does no work and incurs death by Heaven. How so? If a man sits idle all week doing no work, he has nothing to eat on Friday. If he happens to have consecrated money in his house and with this he buys food, he incurs the death penalty [for misappropriating sacred property]. But if as a worker engaged in building the Beis Hamikdash, he was given consecrated money [from the Temple treasury] for his wages, and he used it to buy food, he would not incur death, [because the consecrated money was redeemed when paid out as wages].

R. Dusta'i says: When a man does no work all week he ends up working on Shabbos. Being idle all week with no food for Shabbos, he joins a gang of robbers, and is arrested, taken into custody and forced to work on Shabbos. All this, because he did not work on the six weekdays.

R. Shimon b. Elazar says: Even Adam had nothing to eat before he worked, as it says, *[G-d] placed him in Gan Eden to work it and watch it,* and only then, [G-d says:] *You may definitely eat from every tree of the garden* (*Bereishis* 2:15,16).

R. Tarfon says: The Holy One, blessed be He, also did not allow His *Shechinah* to rest on Yisrael before they did work, as it says, *They shall make Me a sanctuary, and I will dwell among them* (*Shemos* 25:8). From this verse we learn that the men worked, from where do we know the women worked? It says, [Moshe commanded:] *Let no man or woman do more work toward the gift for the Sanctuary*

---

[81] The *vav* of *ve'yom* "and the seventh day" connects Shabbos with the weekdays, to tell you that just as on Shabbos you are required to rest, so are you required to work during the six weekdays. (*Ben Avraham*)

(*Shemos* 36:6). And how do we know the children were involved? The verse ends, *The people* [including children] *stopped bringing.*

R. Nassan says: While Moshe was busy with the work of the Tabernacle, he did not want to consult the tribal leaders of Yisrael. The leaders sat quietly, saying to themselves: "[Let the people bring their contributions, and eventually] Moshe will need our gifts [to complete the Tabernacle, and we will donate the shortfall]." But when they heard the announcement in the camp, *Let no man or woman do more work toward the gift for the Sanctuary,* they cried: "Woe is us that we did not take part in the work of the Tabernacle!" So they quickly added a large gift of their own, as it says, *The tribal leaders brought the shoham* (sardonyx) *stones* (*Shemos* 35:27).

R. Yehudah b. Beseira says: If a man has no work, what should he do? If he has a neglected yard or a weed-choked field, let him tend to it, as it says, *Six days shall you work* (*Shemos* 20:6). Why does the verse continue, *and accomplish all your work?* To include the person who [has no work but] has a neglected yard or field. He should fix it up.

R. Yose says: A man dies only through idleness, as it says, *He breathed his last, and was brought back to his people* (*Bereishis* 49:33).[82] How is that so? If a man had an epileptic seizure while standing on a roof or on top of a tower or building or at the bank of a river and fell to his death, his death is due to idleness and inactivity. [For had he been working he would not have been standing in that place.]

THE MEEK WILL BE EXALTED

2.1 **Despise [positions of] leadership.** What does this imply? A man should not run for a position of leadership; instead let others appoint him to the post, as it says, *Let another praise you,*

---

[82] The Midrash says that Yaakov died before his time. Why did he die prematurely? Because he was idle, since Yosef took care of all his needs (*Ben Avraham*).

not your own mouth; a stranger, not your own lips (*Mishlei* 27:2).

R. Akiva says: To what can one who promotes himself because of his Torah knowledge, be compared? To a carcass dumped on the road; every passerby puts his hand to his nose, turning from it and walking away, as it says, *If you have been scandalously arrogant, or if you have been a schemer, then clap your hand to your mouth* (*Mishlei* 30:32).

Retorted Ben Azzai: Interpret the verse in its context [giving it a positive slant:] If one debases himself for the sake of the Torah, eating dried dates, wearing filthy clothes, and waiting at the door of the Torah academy [to be the first to enter and the last to leave, thus hearing the entire lecture], every passing [student] will say: "This fellow is a fool!" But he will ultimately be a scholar who has mastered the whole Torah.

R. Yose says: Lower yourself, and you will be exalted; exalt yourself and you will be lowered. Whoever exalts himself for his Torah knowledge will be lowered, and whoever lowers himself for the sake of Torah, will be exalted.

3. **Do not develop a close relationship with the government.** What does this imply? One's name should not come to the attention of government officials, because once his name is noticed by government officials, they will focus on him, [lodging false accusations against him], and have him executed, to confiscate all his property. Neither should one cause his fellow to come to the attention of government officials. How might this happen? If one sits in the market and remarks: "May G-d keep on blessing so-and-so. Today [I saw] a hundred oxen, a hundred sheep, and a hundred goats come from his farm!" A police officer may overhear him and report it to the captain. The captain will have [the wealthy farmer's] house surrounded and take all his possessions. About such [talkative] people it says, *If one blesses his friend loudly from early in the morning, it will be a curse for him* (*Mishlei* 27:14).

Another explanation is: One may sit in the market and say: "May G-d continue blessing so-and-so. Today he unloaded so many *kor* of wheat, and so many *kor* of barley into his warehouse." Bandits overhear him, surround his house, and rob him of his wealth. The next morning the man is left with nothing! About such [talkative] people it says, *If one blesses his friend loudly* . . .

Another explanation of: "Do not develop a close relationship," is: Do not be a frequent visitor at the mayor or deputy mayor's office [unless it is urgent business], because these officials mean to rob the Jews.

Another explanation is: One should [try to avoid] being appointed to high office. Although in the beginning the [other officials] cooperate with him, eventually they will frustrate and obstruct him every step of the way.

4. **Avtalyon says: Scholars, be cautious with your words, for you may give a ruling which may not be interpreted according to the teaching of the Torah and incur the penalty of exile and be banished to a place of evil waters [heresy]. Your disciples may also give a ruling in your name which is not according to the Torah and incur the penalty of exile and be banished to a place of evil waters (Avos 1:11).**

What is meant by evil waters? [Mingling with non-Jews,] as it says, *But they mingled with the nations and learned their deeds* (*Tehillim* 106:35).

Another explanation of "evil water" is heresy.

And some say: They may be banished and forced to do hard labor.

CHAPTER TWELVE

⸺◉⸺

LOVE PEACE

1. Hillel and Shammai received the tradition from [Shemaya and Avtalyon]. Hillel says: Be of the disciples of Aharon, loving and pursuing peace, bringing peace between husband and wife, and loving people and bringing them closer to the Torah.

He used to say: He who seeks renown loses his reputation; he who does not increase [his Torah learning] decreases it; he who does not study [Torah] deserves death; and he who exploits the crown of Torah will fade away (Avos 1:12,13).

2. If I am not for myself, who will be for me? And if I am for myself only, what am I? And if not now, when? (Avos 1:14).

3. Love peace. How should one fulfill this? Love peace between man and man in Yisrael, as Aharon did, as it says [concerning Aharon], *The teaching of truth was in his mouth, and injustice was not found on his lips; he walked with Me in peace and with fairness, and turned many away from iniquity* (*Malachi* 2:6).

R. Meir says: Why does it say, *and turned many away from iniquity?* When Aharon walked along the road and met an evil man, he greeted him. Later, if that man wished to commit a transgression, he would say to himself: "Woe is me! How will I face Aharon afterwards? I'll be ashamed, for he greeted me [and will greet me again when he sees me]". As a result, he will not transgress.

When two men fought, Aharon sat with one of them saying: "Son, let me tell you what your friend is doing. He beats his breast and tears his clothing, exclaiming: 'Woe is me! How can I face my friend after treating him so shabbily. I am terribly ashamed of what I did to him.' "

Aharon stayed with him until he removed all resentment from his heart. Then Aharon sat with the other and told him: "Son, let me tell you what your friend is doing. He beats his breast and tears his clothing, exclaiming: 'Woe is me! How can I face my friend after treating him so shabbily. I am terribly ashamed of what I did to him.' "

He would stay with him until he removed all resentment from his heart. When the two men met they would hug and kiss each other. That is why it says [when Aharon's died], *The entire family of Yisrael mourned Aharon for thirty days* (*Bamidbar* 20:29).[83]

MOURNING AHARON'S DEATH

4. Another explanation: Why did all Yisrael—both men and women—mourn Aharon for thirty days [while Moshe was mourned only by the men]? Because it was Moshe's responsibility to judge according to the letter of the law, but Aharon never said to a man or woman: "You have acted improperly." Therefore it says about him, *The entire family of Yisrael mourned Aharon*. By contrast, it says about Moshe, who admonished them with harsh words, *The men of Yisrael mourned Moshe* (*Devarim* 34:8).

Furthermore, many thousands of Jewish children were named after Aharon! For if not for Aharon these children would not have been born. He would reconcile husband and wife [who had been quarreling]; they would have marital relations and name their baby after Aharon.

Some say: The reason it says, *The entire family of Yisrael mourned Aharon for thirty days* is this: [Aharon died before Moshe did, and was mourned by Moshe.] Could anyone see Moshe Rabbeinu sit and weep, and not weep himself? Others say: Could

---

[83] In contrast, Moshe was not as universally mourned, as it says simply, *B'nei Yisrael* mourned Moshe (*Devarim* 34:8), i.e., only the men.

anyone see Elazar and Pinchas [Aharon's son and grandson], two *kohanim gedolim*,[84] weep, and not weep himself!

DEATH OF MOSHE

5. When Aharon died Moshe asked for a death like Aharon's, for he saw Aharon's bier laid out with great honor and a multitude of ministering angels mourning him. Did he make his request in the presence of other people? No, he made his request when he was alone, but the Holy One, blessed be He, heard him whisper, as it says, [Hashem said to Moshe:] *Prepare to die on the mountain that you are climbing and be gathered up to your people, just as your brother Aharon died on Hor Mountain* (*Devarim* 32:49). This teaches us that he asked for a death like Aharon's death.

At that time, G-d said to the angel of death: "Go and bring Me the soul of Moshe." The angel of death went and stood before Moshe. "Moshe, let me have your soul," he demanded.

Moshe scolded him, chasing away indignantly.

Finally, G-d said to Moshe: "Moshe, you have been in this world long enough. The World to Come has been waiting for you since the six days of Creation," as it says, *Hashem then said, "Behold! there is a place with Me; and you will stand on the rock"* (*Shemos* 33:21).

Thereupon, the Holy One, blessed be He, took Moshe's soul, and placed it under the Throne of Glory. Taking the soul, He kissed it, as it says, *Moshe died with Hashem's mouth* (*Devarim* 34:5).

Moshe's soul is not the only soul that is put away under the Throne of Glory. The souls of all the righteous are kept there, as it says, [*Avigail said to David*], *May my lord's soul be bound up in the bond of life in the care of Hashem, your G-d* (1 *Shmuel* 25:29). You might think that the same is true for the wicked. Not so, for the verse

---

[84] Elazar, son of Aharon succeeded his father as *kohen gadol* (*Bamidbar* 20:28); Pinchas was the *kohen mashuach milchamah*, the "kohen anointed for war" (*Sotah* 43a)

continues, *and may He hurl away the soul of your enemies as one shoots a stone from a slingshot.* When you sling [a stone] over a distance you do not know where it will land. So too, the souls of the wicked roam and wander around aimlessly in the world, unable find a resting place.

[Earlier,] the Holy One, blessed be He, had said to the angel of death: "Go and bring Me the soul of Moshe." He went to look for him but could not find him.

So he went to the Great Sea and asked: "Has Moshe been here?"

The Sea replied, "Ever since Yisrael passed through me, I have not seen him."

He went to the mountains and hills and asked: "Have you seen Moshe?" They answered: "Ever since the day Yisrael received the Torah on Mount Sinai, we have nor seen him."

He went to Sheol and Doom, asking: "Have you seen Moshe?" They answered: "We have heard his name, but we have not seen him."

He went to the ministering angels, asking: "Have you seen Moshe?" [They replied,] *"G-d understands his way, only He knows his place"* (*Iyov* 28:23). G-d has set him aside for life in the World to Come, and no one knows [where he is], as it says, *As for wisdom: Where can it be found? Which is the place of understanding? Mankind does not know its worth; it cannot be found in the land of the living. The depth says: "It is not in me!" and the sea says, "It is not with me!" . . . Doom and death say: "With our ears we have heard of its reputation"* (*Iyov* 28:12-15, 22).

Yehoshua too, worried about Moshe, until the Holy One, blessed be He, said: "Yehoshua, why are you concerned about Moshe? *My servant Moshe is dead"* (*Yehoshua* 1:2).

6. [The Mishnah said:] **Pursuing peace.** How should one fulfill this? One should strive to make peace between people [who are quarreling], as it says, *Seek peace and pursue it* (*Tehillim* 34:5).

R. Shimon b. Elazar says: If you sit still, how can you make peace between people? Actively strive for peace in Yisrael, as it says, *Seek peace and pursue it.* Start by making peace in your home town, and [when you have settled all local quarrels,] pursue peace elsewhere.

The Holy One, blessed be He, made peace in heaven. How did He do that? He did not name ten angels Gavriel, ten angels Michael, ten angels Uriel, and ten angels Refael,[85] the way man does. There are [at least] ten people named Reuven, or Shimon, or Levi, or Yehudah. If G-d named angels the way people named people, when He summoned one angel, all [angels with that name] would come running, [and when one angel was sent on a mission] the others would be envious of him. Instead, he named one Gavriel, one Michael. . . Therefore when He calls one of them, only the one He calls comes before Him, and He sends him on whatever mission He wishes.

How do we know that [angels] respect and honor each other and are more humble than man? When they begin to sing, one says to the other: "You begin; you are greater than I," while the other responds: "No, you begin; you are greater than I." This is unlike men, where one says to the other: "I am greater than you," and the other retorts: "No, I am greater than you."

Some say: The angels speak in groups, one group saying to the other: "You begin. You are greater than we," as it says, *And one [group]*[86] *would call to another and say, Holy, holy, holy . . .* (*Yeshayah* 6:3).

7. [The Mishnah said:] Loving people. How should one fulfill this? One should love and not hate people [even if they are wicked].[87] Because the people of the generation of the dispersion[88] loved each other[89] G-d did not wipe them out [although they rebelled against G-d]. Instead, He scattered them to the four

---

[85] These are the four angels that surround the Throne of Glory (*Bamidbar Rabbah* 2)

[86] The preceding verse speaks of *serafim* in the plural. Therefore, *one would call to the other* means one group calling to the other group.

[87] Pray for them that they should repent (*Berachos* 10a).

[88] The generation that built the Tower of Bavel (*Bereishis* 9:1-9)

[89] As it says, *The entire earth had one language and was of common purpose* (*Bereishis* 9:1)

corners of the world. By contrast, the Holy One, blessed be He, annihilated the people of Sedom, in this world and [barred them] from the World to Come, because they hated each other, as it says, *But the people of Sedom were wicked, and they sinned against Hashem very much* (*Bereishis* 13:13).

Wicked toward one another; *and they sinned* refers to immorality; *against Hashem* refers to desecration of G-d's name; *very much*—[they knew G-d,] but intentionally rebelled against Him.

From this we learn that because they hated [and robbed] each other, the Holy One, blessed be He, annihilated them in this world and [barred them] from the World to Come.

8. [**The Mishnah said:**] **Bringing them closer to the Torah.** How should one fulfill this? Persuade people [to overcome their *yetzer hara* (evil impulse)], bringing them under the wings of the Shechinah the way Avraham our father used to persuade people, bringing them under the wings of the Shechinah. Not only did Avraham do this; Sarah also did it, as it says, *Avraham took his wife Sarah, his nephew Lot, and all their belongings, as well as the souls they had made in Charan* (*Bereishis* 12:5). All the people of the world together could not create even a single gnat, so what does the verse, *all the souls they had made in Charan* mean? [By causing them to believe in Hashem] the Holy One, blessed be He, considered it as if [Avraham and Sarah] had made them.

THE REWARD FOR MITZVOS CANNOT BE SHARED

Just as one cannot share the reward [one receives for doing mitzvos with his fellow in this world, because no reward is given for mitzvos in this world], so too, in the World to Come [where the reward for mitzvos is given] one cannot transfer a share of his reward to his fellow, as it says, *Behold! Tears of the oppressed with no one to comfort them, and their oppressors have the power—with no one to comfort them* (*Koheles* 4:1). Why does it say, *with no one to comfort them* twice? This refers to people who eat, drink and prosper with sons and daughters in this world, but have nothing in the World to Come [because they lived only to fulfill their desires. They are punished in Gehinnom,] and *there is no one to comfort them* [for none of their children or relatives comfort them. The phrase is repeated because they are denied the delights of the World to Come, and are also punished in Gehinnom]. In this world, if something is stolen from a person or if one of his relatives dies, his sons, brothers, or relatives comfort him. You might think it will be the same in the World to Come. To teach you otherwise, it says, *He has neither son nor brother* (*Koheles* 4:8) [to redeem him from Gehinnom].

So too, if one commits a transgression, fathering a *mamzer*[90], [the *mamzer*] says to him: "Empty-headed fool! You harmed yourself, and you harmed me." [The twice-mentioned phrase, *there is no one to comfort them* refers to the *mamzer* and his father.] For if a *mamzer* wanted to learn Torah in Yerushalayim, he would be stopped in Ashdod. He would cry, "Woe is me! Were I not a *mamzer* I would be learning [in Yerushalayim] together with my former classmates! But since I am a *mamzer* I cannot join them". For a *mamzer* is strictly forbidden to enter Yerushalayim, as it says, *A* mamzer *will dwell in Ashdod* (*Zechariah* 9:6).[91]

9. [The Mishnah said:] If I am not for myself, who will be for me? If I do not gather merit for myself [by doing mitzvos and good deeds], who will gather it for me?

And if not now, when? If I do not gather merits in my lifetime, who will gather merits for me after I am dead? And so it says, *A live dog is better than a dead lion* (*Koheles* 9:4).

A live dog, refers to the wicked one who is alive in this world. If he does *teshuvah*, G-d accepts him, [and he can gather merit by doing mitzvos].

---

[90] A *mamzer* is someone born of a union between a man and a woman whose marriage could never be valid, such as a union between brother and sister or other forms of incest, or a married woman who bore another man's child.

[91] The Gemara in *Horayot* 13a says that a Torah scholar who is a *mamzer* takes precedence over a *Kohen Gadol*. However, the intense *kedushah* of Yerushalayim does not tolerate a *mamzer*.

A dead lion, refers to Avraham, Yitzchak, and Yaakov for they dwell in the dust. Once the righteous dies he can no longer gather merit.

SAYINGS OF HILLEL

10. [Hillel] used to say: [Hashem says:] "If you come to My house [the *Beis Hamikdash*], I will come to your house; [if you come] to the place My heart loves, My feet lead Me."

What does "If you come to My house, I will come to your house" mean? It refers to those people who come early and stay late in the synagogues and study houses. The Holy One, blessed be He, blesses them, as it says, *Wherever I allow My name to be mentioned, I will come to you and bless you* (*Shemos* 20:21).

What does "To the place My heart loves, My feet lead Me" mean? It refers to those men who leave their silver and gold, going up [to Yerushalayim on the three Yamim Tovim] to greet the *Shechinah* in the Beis Hamikdash. Hashem watches over them while they are encamped [away from home], as it says, *No one will be envious of your land when you go to be seen in Hashem's presence three times a year* (*Shemos* 34:24).

11. [Hillel] used to say: "If I am here, all is here. If I am not here, who is here?"[92] [Ben Bag Bag[93] says:] "Delve in it (the Torah) and continue to delve in it (the Torah) for everything is in it."

---

[92] Rashi *Sukkah* 53a, explains that he is talking in the name of the Shechinah, "As long as My Shechina is in the Bais Hamikdash its glory is intact and Bnei Yisroel will come. However if on account of sin My Shechinah leaves, who will come."

[93] The name Ben Bag Bag, is the acronym for *ben ger ben geyores,* "son of a convert father and convert mother."

[Ben Hei Hei[94] says:] The reward is in proportion to the exertion.

12. One day Hillel, walking along the road, met men carrying wheat.

"How much is a *se'ah*?" he asked.

"Two dinar," they replied.

Then he met others and asked them: "How much is a *se'ah*?"

"Three dinar," they said. "But the other men said a *se'ah* is two *dinar*!" he countered.

"Foolish Babylonian!" they shot back, "don't you know that the reward is in proportion to the exertion, and we carried our wheat over a greater distance; [so we are entitled to more money.]"

"Empty-headed fools!" Hillel replied, "is that the way to answer my question?"

What did Hillel do? He helped them understand the right way, [explaining that the adage applies only to Torah study and mitzvos; not the world of commerce].

G-D PUNISHES MEASURE FOR MEASURE

One day he saw a skull floating on the water; he said to it: "Because you drowned others, they drowned you, and those who drowned you will be eventually drowned (Avos 2:7).

13. He said four more things in Aramaic: **He who seeks renown loses his reputation; he who does not attend the sages deserves to die; he who does not increase his [Torah] learning loses; and he who exploits the crown of Torah shall fade away (Avos 1:13).**

---

94 Ben Hei Hei, means "son of converts" or "son of Avraham and Sarah" to whose names the letter *hei* was added. All converts are named after Avraham, the "father of converts." He is the same as Ben Bag Bag, since Bag (*beis, gimmel* = 2+3) adds up to *hei* (5).

He who seeks renown loses his reputation. What can we learn from this? One's name should not come to the attention of the government. For once one's name is noticed by government officials they focus on him [lodging false accusations against him] having him executed and confiscating all his property.

THE IGNORANT KOHEN

He who does not attend on the sages deserves to die. What does this mean? A man from Beis Ramah was known to lead a saintly life. A disciple whom Rabbi Yochanan b. Zakkai sent to investigate him, found him taking oil, putting it on the range, taking it from the range and pouring it into a dish of beans.

"What are you doing?" the disciple asked.

"I am an adult *kohen*," he replied, "and I eat *terumah*[95] in a state of ritual cleanness."

"Is this range impure or pure?" the disciple asked.

"Does it say anywhere in the Torah about a range being impure?" the *kohen* replied. "The Torah only mentions an oven being impure, as it says, *Anything inside it becomes unclean (Vayikra* 11:33)."[96]

Said the disciple: "Just as the Torah speaks of an oven being impure, so does the Torah speak of a range being pure, as it says, *An oven or a range is impure must be broken down (Vayikra* 11:35).[97]

Concluded the disciple: "If this is how you have led your life, you have never eaten *terumah* that was pure."

---

[95] A farmer must set aside the *terumah* which is about 2% from his crop and give it to a *kohen*. If a *kohen* does not eat the *terumah* in a state of *taharah* (purity), he is liable to die prematurely (*Bamidbar* 18:8, *Devarim* 18:4).

[96] The *kohen* mistakenly thought that only an oven can become impure because it has an inside. He wrongly reasoned that since a range has no inside it cannot become impure.

[97] The verse equates a oven with a range in terms of *tum'ah*.

He who does not increase [his Torah learning] loses. What can we learn from this? If a man learns one, two or three tractates and does not delve deeper into the subjects, he will forget what he has learned.

And he who exploits the crown of Torah shall fade away. What does this mean? Whoever makes use of the Four-Letter Divine name [to perform supernatural feats] has no share in the World to Come.

CHAPTER THIRTEEN

1. Shammai says: Make your Torah study a fixed practice; say little and do much, and receive everyone with a cheerful face. (Avos 1:15)

2. **Make your Torah study a fixed practice.** How should one fulfill this? If you hear something from a sage in the *beis midrash*, do not treat it offhandedly but fix it in your mind. Practice what you learn and teach it to others so that they can do it, as it says, *Learn them and safeguard [the commandments] so you will be able to keep them* (*Devarim* 5:1). Similarly, it says about Ezra, *Ezra set his heart to expounding the Torah of Hashem and fulfilling [its] statute and law in Yisrael* (*Ezra* 7:10).

3. **Say little and do much.** What does this imply? The righteous say little and do much, but the wicked say much and do not even do a little.

How do we know the righteous say little and do much? Avraham our father said to the angels: "You will eat bread with me today," as it says, *I will get a morsel of bread for you to refresh your-selves* (*Bereishis* 18:5). Yet Avraham actually prepared three oxen and nine *se'ah* of fine flour for the ministering angels. How do we know he prepared nine *se'ah* of fine flour for them? It says, *Avraham rushed to Sarah's tent and said, "Hurry, three* se'ah *of the finest flour!"* (*Bereishis* 18:6). [We expound the words calculating:] *Three se'ah*—is taken literally; *flour* makes six; *finest* makes nine.

And from where do we know that he prepared three oxen? It says, *Abraham ran to the cattle, and chose a tender, choice calf* (18:7). *The cattle*—is one; *a calf*—is another; *tender* is three, and some say: *choice* is four.

He gave it to the young man who rushed to prepare it (18:7). [Rather than do the mitzvah himself], he gave it to his son Yishmael to train him in doing mitzvos.

The Holy One, blessed be He, also said little and did much, as it says, *[G-d] said to Avram: "Know for sure that your descendants will be foreigners in a land that is not theirs for four hundred years. They will be enslaved and oppressed. But I will finally bring justice* [dan] *against the nation who enslaves them, and they will then leave with great wealth* (*Bereishis* 15:13,14). G-d promised Avram to bring [the nation] to justice, using the letters *dalet, nun* [dan],[98] but, when He actually retaliated against the enemies of Yisrael, He did so with His [mystical] seventy-two letter name, as it says, *Or has any god ever miraculously come to take for himself a nation from amidst a nation with such tremendous miracles . . . and with greatly awesome deeds* (*Devarim* 4:34).[99] We learn from this that when He retaliates against His enemies, He does so with His 72-letter name.

And how do we know that the wicked say much yet don't even do a little? Efron said to Avraham, *"What's 400 shekels worth of land between you and me? Bury your dead"* [free of charge] (*Bereishis*

---

[98] Alternatively: with the two letters *alef dalet* of the Divine name *A-donay*.

[99] *Midrash Rabbah* (*Vayikra* 23) explains that the phrase, *lavo lakachas lo goy mik-erev goy* until *uvemora'im gedolim* ["come to take for himself a nation . . . until "greatly awesome deeds"] contains 72 letters, excluding the second word "*goy*, na-tion."

23:15). But in the end, Avraham understanding what Efron meant, *weighed out for Efron the silver that had been mentioned* (23:16).

GIVE WITH A SMILE

[The Mishnah said:] And receive everyone with a cheerful face—What does this suggest? If one gives his [needy] neighbor all the good gifts in the world with a sour face, the Torah regards it as though he gave him nothing.[100] But if he greets his [needy] neighbor with a cheerful face [encouraging him and showing compassion,] even though he does not give him anything, the Torah regards it as though he has given him all the good gifts in the world.

CHAPTER FOURTEEN

———◄(●)►———

THE GREATNESS OF RABBI YOCHANAN B. ZAKKAI

1. Rabbi Yochanan b. Zakkai received the tradition from Hillel and Shammai. Hillel the Elder had eighty [primary] disciples, thirty of whom were worthy to have the *Shechinah* rest on them as it did on Moshe Rabbeinu, but their generation was not worthy of it. Thirty of them were worthy to intercalate the years,[101] and the remaining twenty were in between these two levels. The

---

[100] As it says, *Therefore, make every effort to give him, and do not feel bad about giving it* (*Devarim* 15:10).

[101] Adding a second month *Adar* to the year. This had to be done in order to bring the lunar year of 354 days into harmony with the solar year of 365 days, otherwise Pesach would gradually move through the four seasons of the year. Only the most distinguished scholars were appointed to the special court that was convened for that purpose (*Sanhedrin* 10b, 11a).

greatest of them was Rabbi Yonasan b. Uziel, the smallest [of the eighty disciples] was Rabbi Yochanan b. Zakkai.

It was said that Rabbi Yochanan b. Zakkai mastered all of Scripture, Mishnah, Gemara, *halachos, aggados,* exegetical details of the Torah (*dikdukei Torah*) rabbinical enactments (*dikdukei Soferim*), logical deductions (*kal vachomer*), and analogies (*gezeirah shavah*); there was not a single aspect of the Torah that he did not study. [This vast knowledge of Rabbi Yochanan b. Zakkai] is the fulfillment of the verse, *I endow those who love me with substance [i.e., wisdom], and I will fill their treasuries* (*Mishlei* 8:21).

2.ᵢ **(Avos 2:9) He used to say: If you have studied much Torah, do not take credit for yourself, because that is what you were created to do**—for men were created on condition that they study the Torah.

PRAISING HIS DISCIPLES

3.ᵢ Rabbi Yochanan b. Zakkai had five [primary] disciples and he described the attributes of each of them.

He called Rabbi Eliezer b. Hyrkanos, "a cemented cistern that does not lose a drop, a tar-coated flask that keeps its wine."

He called Rabbi Yehoshua b. Chanania, "a three-fold cord that is not quickly broken."

He called Rabbi Yose Hakohen, "the most devout man of the generation."

He called Rabbi Shimon b. Nesanel, "a garden in the desert which holds its water."

He called Rabbi Eliezer b. Arach, "an overflowing stream and a spring which flows stronger and stronger," as it says, *Then your springs will spread outward, streams of water in the thoroughfares* (*Mishlei* 5:16).

4.ᵢ **He used to say: If all the sages of Yisrael were on one pan of a balance-scale, and Rabbi Eliezer b. Hyrkanos were on the other, he would outweigh them all.**

Abba Shaul said in his name: If all the sages of Yisrael, including Rabbi Eliezer b. Hyrkanos, were on one pan of a balance-scale, and Rabbi Elazar b. Arach were on the other, he would outweigh them all (Avos 2:12).

THE PROPER PATH

(Avos 2:13) [Rabbi Yochanan] said to them: Go out and investigate which is the proper way to which a man should cling, thereby entering the World to Come."

Rabbi Eliezer said: A good eye.

Rabbi Yehoshua said: A good friend [who admonishes you when you do wrong].

Rabbi Yose said: A good neighbor, a good inclination, and a good wife.

Rabbi Shimon said: One who considers the outcome of a deed.

Rabbi Elazar [b. Arach] said: A good heart toward heaven and toward one's fellowmen.

[Rabbi Yochanan b. Zakkai] said to them: I prefer the words of Rabbi Elazar b. Arach to your words, for your words are included in his words.

5. He then said to them: Go out and investigate the evil way a person should avoid, so he may enter the World to Come.

Rabbi Eliezer said: An evil eye.

Rabbi Yehoshua said: A bad friend.

Rabbi Yose said: a bad neighbor, an evil inclination, and a bad wife.

Rabbi Shimon said: One who borrows and does not repay, for borrowing from man is like borrowing from G-d, as it says, *The wicked one borrows and does not repay, but the Righteous One is gracious and gives* (*Tehillim* 37:21).

Rabbi Elazar ben Arach said: A wicked heart towards heaven, towards mitzvos and towards his fellow man.

[Rabbi Yochanan b. Zakkai] said to them: I prefer the words of
Rabbi Elazar b. Arach to your words, for your words are included
in his words.

COMFORTING THEIR MASTER

6. When Rabbi Yochanan b. Zakkai's son died, his disciples
came to comfort him. Rabbi Eliezer entered, and sitting
before him, said:

"Rebbi, with your permission, I would like to say something."

"Speak," he replied.

Said Rabbi Eliezer: "Adam had a son who died, and he accepted words of consolation about him. How do we know this?
Because it says, *Adam knew his wife again* (*Bereishis* 4:25). May
you, too, be comforted."

Said Rabbi Yochanan: "Is it not enough that I am mourning for
my own loss? Must you remind me of the grief of Adam?"

Rabbi Yehoshua entered and said:

"Rebbi, with your permission, I would like to say something."

"Speak," Rabbi Yochanan replied.

Said Rabbi Yehoshua: "Iyov had sons and daughters all of whom
died in one day, and he accepted words of consolation about them.
May you, too, be comforted." How do we know Iyov accepted
words of consolation? Because Iyov said, *Hashem has given, and
Hashem has taken away, blessed be the name of Hashem* (*Iyov* 1:21).

Said Rabbi Yochanan: "Is it not enough that I am mourning for
my own loss? Must you remind me of the grief of Iyov?"

Rabbi Yose entered, sat before him, and said:

"Rebbi, with your permission, I would like to say something."

"Speak," he replied.

Said Rabbi Yose: "Aharon had two distinguished sons both of
whom died in one day, and he accepted words of consolation about
them, for it says, *Aharon remained silent* (*Vayikra* 10:3), and si-
lence means consolation. May you, too, be comforted."

Said Rabbi Yochanan: "Is it not enough that I am mourning for my own loss? Must you remind me of the grief of Aharon?"

Rabbi Shimon entered and said: "Rebbi, with your permission, I would like to say something."

"Speak," Rabbi Yochanan replied.

Said Rabbi Shimon: "King David had a son who died, and he accepted words of consolation. How do we know he accepted words of consolation? Because it says, *David comforted his wife Bas-sheva, and he came to her and lay with her; and she bore him a son and called his name Shlomoh* (2 *Shmuel* 12:24). May you, too, be comforted."

Said Rabbi Yochanan: "Is it not enough that I am mourning for my own loss? Must you remind me of the grief of King David?"

Rabbi Elazar b. Arach entered. When Rabbi Yochanan b. Zakkai saw him, he said to his attendant: "Take my clothing and follow me to the bathhouse, for he is a great man and [surely he will be able to comfort me] so I can end my [mourning]."[102]

Rabbi Elazar sat down before him and said: "Let me tell you a parable: To what can [your loss] be compared? To a man whom the king entrusted with a precious article for safekeeping. Every day the man wept, crying out: 'Woe is me! I wish for the day that I can return this deposit in peace!' Rebbi, you, had a son, who mastered the Torah, the Prophets, the Writings, Mishnah, Halachah, and Aggadah, and he left the world without sin. May you be comforted, because you have given back [the soul] that was entrusted to you in an immaculate state."

Replied Rabbi Yochanan: "Rabbi Elazar, my son, you have comforted me the way all men should express sympathy."

When [the five disciples] left, Rabbi Elazar b. Arach said: "I will go to Diumsis (Emmaus),"[103]—a resort with wonderful and healthful water.

[He assumed his colleagues would follow him] but they said: "We will go to Yavneh, where there are a great number of Torah scholars who love the Torah."

---

[102] Although bathing is forbidden during the mourning period, he was permitted to bathe because he was very frail and delicate.

[103] A town in the plain of Judea renowned for its warm springs and luxurious life.

Because he went to the luxurious spa of Diumsis, his standing in Torah learning diminished;[104] [From being the greatest of the five disciples, he declined, with his name occurring only a few times in the entire Talmud, whereas his colleagues' names are mentioned almost on every page.] Their names are prevalent in the Torah because they went to Yavneh where there is an abundance of scholars who love the Torah.

CHAPTER FIFTEEN

1.
They[105] each said **three things** [on the subject of ethics].

Rabbi Eliezer says: Let your fellow's honor be as dear to you as your own; do not anger easily; and Repent one day before your you die (Avos 2:15).

Let your fellow's honor be as dear to you as your own. How should one fulfill this? Just as you value your own honor, so should you value your fellow's honor. And just as no one wants a slur cast on his own honor, so should he make sure no slur is cast on his fellow's honor.

Another explanation for: "Let your fellow's honor be as dear to you as your own"—Just as a man will not violate his fellow's honor if he has millions, so too, [he should not lower his standards,] making sure not to violate his fellow's honor, even if all his wealth is taken away.

---

104 The Gemara in *Shabbos* 147b relates an instance where he even forgot how to read correctly from the Torah. Eventually, Eliyahu Hanavi retaught him all the Torah he had forgotten.

105 Each of the five disciples mentioned in the previous chapter.

HILLEL'S INFINITE PATIENCE

2.1 **Do not anger easily.** One should be patient like Hillel the Elder, rather than short-tempered like Shammai the Elder. How great was the patience of Hillel the Elder?

Two men made a wager, saying: The one who makes Hillel angry will receive four hundred *zuz*. One said: "I'll go and make him angry." On Friday afternoon, when Hillel was washing his head, the man knocked on his door, [disrespectfully] shouting, "Where's Hillel? Where's Hillel?" [without mentioning Hillel's title of *Nasi*]. Hillel put on his robe and came out, saying [calmly]: "My son, how can I help you?"

"I have a question to ask," he replied.

"Go ahead and ask," said Hillel.

"Why are the heads of the Babylonians long?" inquired the man.

"My son you have asked a very important question," replied Hillel. "It is because they don't have good midwives. When a baby is born it is cared for by slaves and maid-servants who hold the baby on their laps, therefore their heads are long. However here, we have skilled midwives, who place the newborn baby in a cradle, and rub its head, therefore, here the heads are round."

The man left, waited a while, then came back and called out: "Where's Hillel? Is Hillel here?" Hillel put on his robe and came out.

"My son," he said gently, "what can I do for you?"

"I have a question to ask."

"Ask, my son."

"Why are the Tarmodians weak-eyed?"

"My son, you have asked an astute question," he answered. "Because they live in the desert, and the wind is forever blowing sand into their eyes."

The man left, waited a while, then came back and called out: "Is Hillel here? Where's Hillel?"

Hillel put on his robe and came out.

"My son what can I do for you this time?"

"I have a question to ask."

"Ask, my son."

"Why do the Africans have wide feet?"

"My son, you have asked an important question," said Hillel.

"They live in marshy places, [and because of their wide feet they do not sink into the swamp.]"

[Desperate because he was losing the wager], the man said: "I have many more such questions to ask, but I'm afraid that you are going to get angry with me."

Hillel put on his robe, sat down and said: "Ask all the questions you want to ask."

Said he: "Are you the Hillel who is called *Nasi* (Prince, Leader) of Yisrael?"

"Yes, I am."

"If you are really he," the man retorted, "may there not be any more like you in Yisrael."

"Why, my son?"

"I lost 400 *zuz* because of you!" the man exclaimed.

Replied Hillel: "Always be careful and watch your temper. It is better that you lose 400 *zuz* because of Hillel, and even another 400 *zuz*, than Hillel should lose his temper."

HILLEL CONVINCES THE NON-JEW

3. How strict was Shammai the Elder? Someone approached Shammai asking him: "Rabbi, how many Torahs do you have?"

Shammai replied: "We have two: the Written and the Oral Torah."

Said the man: "I believe you regarding the Written Torah, but not regarding the Oral Torah."

Shammai scolded him, sending him away in disgust.

He then went to Hillel and asked him: "How many Torahs do you have?"

Hillel replied: "We have two: the Written and the Oral Torah."

"I believe you regarding the Written Torah, but not regarding the Oral Torah," the man answered.

"Sit down, my son," Hillel said soothingly. He then wrote down the entire *alef beis* [and taught him it to him. The next day, pointing to one of the letters,] Hillel asked: "What is this?"

"That's an *alef*," the man said confidently.

Said Hillel: "No, that's not an *alef*; that's a *beis!*"

[Pointing to another letter,] Hillel asked: And what's this?"

"A *beis*,"

"That's not a *beis*," Hillel said, "that's a *gimmel!*"

Bewildered, the man said: "But yesterday you taught me differently!"

Hillel explained, "[Of course, you read the letters correctly.] But how do we know that this is an *alef* and that is a *beis*? Because our ancestors told us. Just as you accept this, so must you trust [that the Oral Torah is a tradition we received from G-d].

A Convert Desires to Become *Kohen Gadol*

Once a non-Jew passed behind a *beis midrash*, and overheard a child reciting the verse, *These are the garments that they shall make: a breastplate and an efod*[106] (*Shemos* 28:4).

He asked Shammai: " For whom are all these glorious garments?"

"For the *Kohen Gadol* who conducts the service at the altar," Shammai replied.

Said the non-Jew: "Convert me on condition that you appoint me *Kohen Gadol.*"

"Do the Jewish People lack their own *kohanim?*" burst out, Shammai. "Don't we have our own *Kohen Gadol* to perform the service? Do we need a common convert who comes with no more than his staff and bag to officiate as *Kohen Gadol?!*" Shammai scolded him, angrily sending him away.

---

[106] The *efod* was a half-cape as wide as the body, reaching from just below the elbows to the heel, that was worn by the *Kohen Gadol* (High Priest). It had a belt that was tied in front, and two shoulder straps.

The non-Jew went to Hillel [with the same request]. "Sit down," Hillel said graciously, "and let me tell you something. If one wants an audience with a king of flesh and blood, shouldn't he know the etiquette of entering and leaving [the palace]?"

"Yes."

"So too, if you want an audience with the King of kings, the Holy One, blessed be He, surely you must know how to enter the Holy of Holies, how to prepare the lights of the Menorah, how to offer the sacrifices on the Altar, how to arrange the Table [of the showbreads], and how to lay out the pile of wood [on which to burn the sacrifices]."

"Do what you think is right," the man replied humbly.

Hillel began teaching him the *alef beis.* Then he taught him the book of *Vayikra* [which contains most of the laws relating to priesthood]. The man continued learning until he came to the verse, *Any stranger [who is not a kohen] that comes close shall die"* (*Bamidbar* 1:51). He drew a logical conclusion: If the Torah says about the people of Israel—who are called children of the Almighty, and *a kingdom of priests and a holy nation to Me* (*Shemos* 19:6)—*Any stranger [who is not a kohen] who comes close shall die,* surely this applies to a common convert who comes with his staff and his bag. This thought immediately gave him peace of mind.

He said to Hillel the Elder: "May all the blessing of the Torah rest on your head. Had you been like Shammai the Elder I would not have entered the community of Israel. The quick temper of Shammai almost caused me to perish from this world and from the World to Come. Your patience brought me to life in the World to Come."

Two sons were born to this convert; one he named Hillel and the other he named Gamliel,[107] and they were called "the converts of Hillel."

---

[107] the grandson of Hillel.

4. **[We learned in the Mishnah:] Repent one day before you die.** Rabbi Eliezer's students asked him: Does anyone know when he will die [in order to do *teshuvah* the day before]?

Replied Rabbi Eliezer: "All the more reason that he should repent today, since he might die tomorrow, and he should repent tomorrow for he may die the next day. Thus, he will spend his whole life in *teshuvah*."

Rabbi Yose b. Yehudah says in the name of Rabbi Yehudah b. Ila'i, who said in the name of his father, Rabbi Ila'i, who said in the name of Rabbi Eliezer the Great: **Repent one day before you die; warm yourself by the fire of the sages, but beware of their glowing coal lest you be burnt—for their bite is the bite of a fox, their sting is the sting of a scorpion, and all their words are like fiery coals (Avos 2:15).**

CHAPTER SIXTEEN

THE SCOURGE OF ENVY

1. **Rabbi Yehoshua says: An evil eye, the evil impulse, and hatred of other people put a man out of the world. (Avos 2:16)**

What is "an evil eye"? Just as a man is happy when things go well for him, so should he be happy when things go well for his neighbor. And just as a man hates if his wife and children are maligned, so should he hate hearing his neighbor's wife and children maligned.

Another explanation of "an evil eye"—One should not envy his fellow's learning. A man who was envious of his friend's learning had his life cut short, and he passed away.

THE *YETZER HARA*

2. **The evil impulse:** The Sages said a man's evil impulse is thirteen years older than his good impulse. [When the fetus emerges] from his mother's womb the evil impulse begins to develop[108] staying with a person from his very beginning. [This explains why a person listens to the enticements of the *yetzer hara*]. [If the *yetzer hara*] incites a person to desecrate the Shabbos or adultery, there is no [counterforce] to prevent him from sinning.

Thirteen years later the good impulse is born. If a person is about to desecrate the Shabbos, the *yetzer tov* admonishes him, "Rascal! Don't you know it says, *Anyone violating [the Shabbos] shall be put to death!*" (*Shemos* 31:14). If he wishes to commit murder, the *yetzer tov* admonishes him. "Rascal! Don't you know that it says, *He who spills human blood shall have his own blood spilled by man!*" (*Bereishis* 9:6). If he wishes to commit adultery, the *yetzer tov* admonishes him. "Rascal! Don't you know that it says, *Both the adulterer and the adulteress shall be put to death!*" (*Vayikra* 20:10).

When a man lusts to commit a promiscuous act, his limbs obey him, for the *yetzer hara* is king over his 248 limbs. When he does a mitzvah his limbs slow him down for the same reason. Indeed, the *yetzer tov* is like a captive in prison, as the verse referring to the *yetzer tov* says: *Because from prison he emerged to reign (Koheles 4:14)*. Others say this verse refers to *Yosef Hatzaddik*.

YOSEF'S VIRTUE

When [Potifar's wife] that wicked woman, tried to seduce Yosef [and he rejected her advances], she said:

"I will lock you in prison."

He retorted: *"G-d sets prisoners free"* (*Tehillim* 146:7).

She said: "I will blind your eyes."

---

[108] As it says, *Sin rests at the door* (*Bereishis* 4:7), and *For the inclination of man's heart is evil from his youth* (*Bereishis* 8:21).

He replied: "*G-d restores sight to the blind*" (146:8).

She said: "I will bend your proud stature [i.e., disgrace you]."

He shot back: "*G-d makes those who are bent, stand straight*" (146:8).

She said: "I will force you to do wicked things."

He answered: "*G-d loves the righteous*" (146:8).

She said: "I will force you to become a pagan."

He said: "*G-d watches over the strangers*" (146:9)

At last he said: "*How could I do such a great wrong? It would be a sin before G-d*" (*Bereishis* 39:9).

THE SAINTLINESS OF THE SAGES

Don't be surprised at Yosef Hatzaddik's virtue, for the story of [the temptation of] Rabbi Tzadok is more surprising.[109] When he was taken captive to Rome, a prominent lady acquired him [as a slave]. She sent a beautiful slavegirl to be with him. When he saw her approaching, he turned toward the wall in order not to look at her. All night he sat and studied. In the morning the slavegirl complained to her mistress. "I'd rather die, than be given to this man." The lady sent for him and asked: "Why didn't you do with this woman what men usually do?"

"What could I do?" he replied. "I am from a respected family of high priests". I said to myself: "If I come to her, I will bring illegitimate children into Israel."

Hearing this she ordered [that he be set free], and he was sent off with great honor.

Don't be amazed at Rabbi Tzadok's chastity, for the story of Rabbi Akiva's purity is even more astonishing. While in Rome he was slandered before a certain governor. The governor sent two beautiful women to him. They were bathed, anointed and adorned

---

[109] Although Rabbi Tzadok was not as saintly a man as Yosef, he resisted an equally strong temptation.

like brides. All night long they made advances to him, this one begging: "Come to me," and the other one begging: "Come to me."
Disgusted, he snubbed them. They left and angrily complained to
the governor: "We'd rather die than be given to this man!"

The governor sent for him. "Why didn't you do with these
women what men usually do with women? Are they not attractive?
Are they not human beings like yourself? Did not He who created
you, create them?"

"I could not help it," Rabbi Akiva replied, "I was repelled by
their bad breath; [caused by] the non-kosher animals and creeping
things they had eaten."

Don't be astonished by Rabbi Akiva's purity, for the story of
Rabbi Eliezer the Great is even more amazing. For thirteen years
he raised his sister's daughter, and she slept with him in the same
bed until signs of puberty appeared. Then he said to her: "Go and
get married."

She replied: "Your maidservant is merely a handmaid to wash
the feet of your disciples."[110]

"My child," he answered, "I am an old man. Go and marry a
young man your own age."

"But I already told you," she replied, "your maidservant is
merely a handmaid to wash the feet of your disciples."

Understanding what she implied, he asked to marry her,[111] and
[he married her] and came to her.

YETZER HARA ENTERS AT BIRTH

3. Rabbi Reuven ben Atztroboli said: How [careful must] a
man [be to] avoid [being trapped by] the *yetzer hara* which
resides inside him! For the first drop of semen a man puts into a

---

[110] Hinting that she wanted to marry Rabbi Eliezer, using the phrase by which
Abigail indicated that she wanted to marry David (1 *Shmuel* 25:41).
[111] A woman must give her consent to be married (*Kiddushin* 2a).

woman contains the *yetzer hara,* which lies exactly at the opening of the heart, as it says, *Sin is crouching at the door* [of the heart] (*Bereishis* 4:7). The [*yetzer hara*] terrifies a person from the time he is an infant lying in his cradle, telling him such things as: "A man who will pull out your hair and kill you is coming!" It is the *yetzer hara* that makes a baby in his crib reach for a snake or scorpion and then be bitten. It is the yetzer hara that makes a baby reach for hot coals causing him to be burned. [Should you argue that a baby gets hurt because his mind is not yet developed to sense danger,] observe a newborn kid or lamb; when it sees a pit it pulls back [to avoid falling in], because animals do not have a *yetzer hara.*

4. Rabbi Shimon b. Elazar said a parable explaining [how to deal with the *yetzer hara.*] The *yetzer hara* can be compared to a bar of iron that is held in a flame. As long as it is in the flame, it can be shaped into any object one wishes. So too, the *yetzer hara* can be subdued through the words of the Torah which are like fire, as it says, *If your foe is hungry, feed him bread; and if he is thirsty, give him water to drink, for you will be scooping coals [to heap] on his head, and Hashem will reward you* (*Mishlei* 25:21,22). The words *yeshalleim lach*—will reward you, should be read *yashlim lach*— will be at peace with you[112] [meaning the words of the Torah will cause the *yetzer hara* to become your friend.]

Rabbi Yehudah Hanasi (the Prince) says: Let me explain it with this parable: The *yetzer hara* can be compared to two men who enter an inn. [The police] arrest one man for robbery asking him: "Who is your partner?" Though he could answer: "I have no partner", he says to himself: "If I am to be killed, let my partner be killed with me." Similarly, the *yetzer hara* says: "Since I don't have a chance of entering the World to Come, I'll destroy the whole body."[113]

---

[112] Bread, water, and fire symbolize the Torah. The arch-enemy—the *yetzer hara*— can be conquered only through the Torah. When you live by the Torah, the *yetzer hara* will be defeated, becoming your friend, and no longer make you sin.

[113] The *yetzer hara* is identical to Satan and the *Malach Hamaves* (the Angel of Death).

Said R. Shimon b. Yocha'i: The righteous will never see the inside of Gehinnom. This can be compared to a king who had an unproductive field. People rented the field for ten *kor* wheat per year. They fertilized it, plowed it, watered it, and cultivated it, but took in no more than one *kor* of wheat [which they gave to the king as rent].

"What happened?" the king asked.

"Your majesty!" they replied, "Until now the field you gave us produced nothing at all. Now after fertilizing, cultivating and watering it, we were only able to harvest one *kor* of wheat."

So too, in time to come, Yisrael will plead before the Holy One, blessed be He: "Master of the universe, The *yetzer hara* seduces us [trying to lead us astray completely, but at least we fulfilled some of the mitzvos. Please do not hold it against us that we did not keep all the mitzvos as we promised to do]," as it says, *For He knows our* yetzer (*inclination*)" (*Tehillim* 103:14).

5. [The Mishnah said:] And hatred of other people [puts a man out of this world]. One should not say: "Love the Sages, but hate the disciples;" or "Love the Sages but hate the ignorant." On the contrary, love everyone, only hating the heretics,[114] those who entice others to go astray, those who worship other gods, and informers, as David said, *For those who hate You, O Hashem, I hate, and I quarrel with those who rise up against You. With the utmost hatred I hate them; they have become enemies to me* (*Tehillim* 139:21,22).

It says, *You must love your neighbor as [you love] yourself, I am Hashem* (Vayikra 19:18), teaching that if one acts as a Jew you must love him, but if he does not, you should not love him.

Rabbi Shimon b. Elazar says: The statement, *You must love your neighbor as [you love] yourself* was followed by the strong warning: *I am Hashem*—[implying,] that if you love him I am faithful to richly reward you; but if not, I am the judge to punish.

---

[114] One who denigrates a Torah scholar, or one who denigrates his fellow in the presence of a Torah scholar (*Sanhedrin* 99b).

CHAPTER SEVENTEEN

---==•===---

LOVE YOUR NEIGHBOR

1. Rabbi Yose says: Let your fellow's money be as dear to you as your own; apply yourself to Torah study for it is not yours by inheritance, and let all your deeds be for the sake of Heaven (Avos 2:17).

2. Let your fellow's money be as dear to you as your own, teaches that just as you are careful not to lose your own money, so must you make sure your fellow does not lose his money; and just as no one wishes that false aspersions be cast on his money [suggesting it was stolen, or acquired through cheating or interest], so should he make sure no false aspersions are cast on his fellow's money.

Another interpretation: When a poor man enters your home, give him money immediately if you have, and send him on his way. Do not delay him, as it says, *Do not say to your fellow, "Come back again; I'll give it to you tomorrow," when you have it with you* (*Mishlei* 3:28).

3. Apply yourself to Torah study for it is not yours by inheritance: [Don't say: Since my father and ancestors were Torah scholars, I will inherit their learning without studying.] When Moshe saw that his sons [relying on his merit,] did not apply themselves to Torah and therefore might not succeed him as leaders, he wrapped himself in his cloak, praying: "Master of the universe, let me know who will lead this people." As it says, *Moshe spoke to Hashem, saying, "Let the omnipotent G-d of all living souls appoint a man over the community. Let him come and go before them"* (*Bamidbar* 27:15-17).

Replied the Holy One, blessed be He, "*Take Yehoshua* (27:18). Establish an interpreter for him, letting him expound the law to the great sages of Yisrael in your presence, [so no one will question his authority]."

At that point Moshe said to Yehoshua: "Yehoshua, this people which I am handing over to you are not goats, but kids; they are not sheep, but lambs, for they are not well-versed in the commandments, and they have not yet become full-grown goats and sheep." As it says, *If you do not know, O fairest of women, go follow the tracks of the sheep, and graze your kids by the tents of the shepherds* (*Shir Hashirim* 1:8).

THE TRAGIC PLIGHT OF NAKDIMAN'S DAUGHTER

4. [Rabbi Yochanan b. Zakkai applied the above mentioned verse to the following story.]

Rabbi Yochanan b. Zakkai [who lived during the dreadful time of the destruction of the Beis Hamikdash] was in the market when he saw a [starving] young woman picking barley grains out of the dung of Arab cattle.

"My daughter," he asked her, "Who are you?" She did not answer. Again he asked her: "My daughter, who are you?" and again she did not answer.

Finally she said: "Wait a moment." Covering her hair she stood in front of him and said, "Rabbi, I am the daughter of Nakdiman b. Gurion[115]."

"What happened to your father's fortune?" he asked.

"Rabbi," she answered, "don't they have a saying in Yerushalayim: One salts wealth by decreasing" [meaning, you preserve your wealth by decreasing it through giving charity. She implied that her father did not give enough *tzedakah*]. Others say,

---

[115] One of the wealthiest men in Yerushalayim.

"One salts wealth by benevolence," [meaning, you preserve your wealth by doing kind deeds.]

Rabbi Yochanan b. Zakkai then asked: "And what happened to your father-in-law's wealth?" She replied: "One destroyed the other" [i.e., the two fortunes were linked to each other, and when one was lost the other went down with it.]

At this, Rabbi Yochanan said to his disciples: "All my life I have read this verse, *If you do not know, O fairest of women, go follow the tracks of the sheep,* and only today did I understand what it meant:[116] Yisrael was handed over to the lowliest of nations, and not just to the lowliest of nations but to the dung of their cattle."

She continued: "Rabbi, do you remember when you signed my *kesubah* (marriage contract)?" He replied, "I remember". Turning to his disciples he said: "When I signed her *kesubah* I read that her father gave her thousands upon thousands of gold coins, in addition to the amount she received from her father-in-law. In the prosperous days of this young woman's father, they did not go from their house to the Beis Hamikdash unless a carpet of fine wool was laid for them to walk on!"

Captive Girls

5. A young girl was taken captive together with her ten maid-servants. A Greek bought them, and she was brought up as a member of his household. One day he handed her a pitcher, saying: "Go and bring me water." Instantly one of her maidservants jumped up and took it from her. "What is the meaning of this?" he wanted to know.

"I swear, Sir," she replied, "I was one of five hundred maid-servants of this girl's mother."

Upon hearing this he set the girl free together with her ten maidservants.

---

[116] The interpretation: If the Jewish nation does not keep the Torah, they will be driven into exile to live under the dominance of the uncivilized Arabs.

6. Another young girl was taken captive, and bought by a certain Greek who raised her as a member of his household. The heavenly master of dreams appeared to the Greek and said: "Send this girl away from your house!"

But his wife told him: "Don't send her away."

The heavenly master of dreams appeared to him again and said: "If you don't send her away, I will kill you." He sent her away, but followed behind her saying to himself, "I will see what will become of this girl."

Walking along the road she grew thirsty, so she climbed down a slope to drink water from a spring. As she leaned against the wall [around the spring], a snake bit her. She died instantly and lay floating on the water. [The Greek] grabbed her, and lifting her [out of the water], buried her. Arriving home he told his wife: "This people [suffers so much] only because their Father in heaven is angry with them."

7. [The Mishnah said:] And let all your deeds be for the sake of heaven—for the sake of Torah, as it says, *In all your ways know Him, and He will smooth your paths* (*Mishlei* 3:6). [Even when engaged in mundane activities like eating, drinking and taking a walk your intention should be to gain strength to enable you serve G-d].

8. Rabbi Shimon says: Be meticulous in reading the Shema and in prayer [i.e., the *Shemoneh esrei*]; when you pray, do not make your prayer a set routine, but rather [beg for] compassion before the Omnipotent, as it says, *You are a gracious and merciful G-d, slow to anger, abundant in kindness, and relent from doing harm* (*Yonah* 4:3) (Avos 2:18).

Rabbi Elazar says: Be diligent in the study of Torah and know what to answer a heretic. Do not forget one word of the Torah. Know before whom you toil, and know [that the Almighty] made the covenant with you, and will reward you for your [good] works (Avos 2:19).

CHAPTER EIGHTEEN

―――≈◉≈―――

VIRTUES OF FIVE SAGES

1. Following the example [of Rabbi Yochanan who described the individual teaching methods of his disciples in chapter 14:3], Rabbi Yehudah Hanasi (the Prince) identified the distinctive approach to learning of the following sages: Rabbi Tarfon, Rabbi Akiva, Rabbi Elazar b. Azariah, Rabbi Yochanan b. Nuri, and Rabbi Yose Hagelili.

He called Rabbi Tarfon "a pile of stones" or, some say, "a pile of nuts", for when you remove one from the pile, they all tumble down on top of each other. When a Torah scholar asked Rabbi Tarfon, "Please explain [a certain halachic point] to me," Rabbi Tarfon's [answers came in a torrent, like a collapsing heap of nuts.[117]] He quoted [all relevant sources in] Scripture, Mishnah, Midrash, Halachah and Aggadah. When the scholar left, he went away filled with blessing and goodness.

He called Rabbi Akiva "a neatly arranged warehouse," [his learning was broken down into clearly defined areas of study]. To what can Rabbi Akiva be compared? To a laborer who [looked for work] carrying his basket. When he found [a job harvesting] wheat he was paid with wheat which he put in the basket; when he was paid with barley he put that in the basket; when he was paid with spelt he placed it in the basket; when he was paid beans and lentils, he put those in his basket. At home, he sorted the wheat, the barley, the spelt, the beans, and the lentils.[118] Thus Rabbi Akiva cate-

---

[117] Rashi on *Gittin* 67a.
[118] The five species: wheat, barley . . . correspond to the five areas of learning: Scripture, Mishnah, Midrash, Halachah, and Aggadah. He received his knowledge from his masters as a blend of the various fields of study, but he taught the material to his students in an organized fashion.

gorized [the subject matter when teaching his students, separating the five areas of study], arranging the whole Torah in rings [i.e., individual themes].[119]

He called Rabbi Elazar b. Azariah a spice-peddler's basket; [meaning, he had his answers readily available]. To what can Rabbi Elazar be compared? To a spice-peddler in a city carrying his wares in his case. When the townsfolk asked him: "Do you carry good oil? Do you carry fragrant ointment? Do you carry balsam?" they found that he carried everything with him. Similarly when a scholar asked Rabbi Elazar b. Azariah a question about Scripture, he had an answer; so too, he answered questions on Mishnah; questions on Halachah, and question on Aggadah. When the scholar left he went away filled with blessing and goodness.

RABBI ELAZAR B. AZARIAH'S TEACHINGS

2. In Rabbi Yehoshua's old age his disciples visited him regularly. One day he asked them: "My children, what new teaching have you learned in the *beis midrash* today?"

"We are your disciples," they replied, "and it is your waters we drink". [Disciples may not speak before their teacher (Rashi); besides, we cannot possibly tell you a novel thought. You know everything there is to know.]

"Heaven forbid!" he exclaimed. ["I am giving you permission to speak.] There is no generation without sages. [Surely there were interpretations given, of which I am not aware]. Tell me, whose Shabbos was it?"[120]

"It was the Shabbos of Rabbi Elazar b. Azariah," they replied.

"On what chapter did he expound?" Rabbi Yehoshua inquired.

"He lectured on the verse, *You must gather together the people, the men, women, and children . . . (Devarim 31:12).*

---

[119] See Rashi *Gittin* 67a.
[120] Rabbi Elazar b. Azariah used to lecture one Shabbos every month, Rabban Gamliel lectured on the other three.

"And how did he explain it?"

"This is how he expounded: The men come to learn, the women to hear, but why do the children come? In order to bestow [heavenly] reward on [the mothers] who bring them."

Said Rabbi Yehoshua: "You held a precious pearl in your hand, and you wanted to deprive me of it! Had you come only to tell me this [interpretation], your visit would have been worthwhile."

They said: "He also expounded the verse, *The sayings of the wise are like goads, and like nails well driven are the sayings of the masters of assemblies. They are all given from one Shepherd* (*Koheles* 12:11). Just as a goad guides the cow [pulling the plow] along the furrow, so do the words of the Torah guide man along the way of life. But [lest you think] the words of the Torah are unstable like a goad which is movable, the verse continues, *as nails well driven*. Just as nails that are well driven cannot be removed, so are the words of the Torah well driven and unable be removed.

The masters of assemblies [mentioned in the above verse] are the Torah scholars who come [to the yeshivah] sitting in groups: some forbid and others permit, some pronounce a thing unclean, others pronounce it clean, some disqualify [a person as a witness or kohen[121]], others declare him fit. About a person who says, ["Since the scholars cannot agree,] I will not learn Torah", it says, *They are all given from one Shepherd*. One G-d gave [the laws], one leader [Moshe] transmitted them, the Master of all creation uttered them.[122] Funnel your ears and take in the words of those that forbid and those that permit, those that pronounce unclean and those that pronounce clean, those that disqualify and those that declare fit.

[Rabbi Yehudah] called Rabbi Yochanan b. Nuri, "a basket of halachos."

He called Rabbi Yose Hagelili: "A talented collector of Torah insights [gathering insights even from less important scholars, for he

---

121 Rashi on Chagigah 3b.
122 I.e., The various opinions do not emanate from different "revelations;" they originate in the Torah given by One G-d.

is], free of haughtiness." He learned the quality [of humility] from Mount Sinai [which G-d chose as the site to give the Torah because it was the lowest mountain], and he instilled [this quality] in all the sages of Yisrael.

3. Isi b. Yehudah also coined phrases illustrating the distinctive merits of the various sages.

Rabbi Meir [he said] is wise and a scribe;[123]

Rabbi Yehudah [he described as] wise when he wishes to be, [implying that when he is not too hasty he is even wiser than Rabbi Meir (*Tosafos*);]

Rabbi Eliezer b. Yaakov is small but flawless. [He authored few halachos, but wherever he gives an opinion the halachah is according to him];

Rabbi Yose always has a valid reason to uphold his views;

Rabbi Yochanan b. Nuri: a basket of halachos;

Rabbi Yose Hagelili: a talented gatherer of Torah insights, free from haughtiness;

Rabbi Shimon b. Gamliel: a fully stocked store, [he is well-versed in any subject, ready to answer any question on the spot].

Rabbi Shimon (b. Yocha'i) learns a great deal and forgets little.

One day Rabbi Shimon, meeting Isi b. Yehudah asked, "Why do you humiliate me in front of the sages, [saying that I forget some things?]"

Isi answered: "I said you learn a great deal, and forget little and the little you do forget is the bran of your learning"—meaning it is the part that is not accepted as halachah (Rashi)]."

---

123 This was his profession, Sotah 20a.

CHAPTER NINETEEN

---◆---

REFLECTIONS ON MAN'S DESTINY

1. Akavyah ben Mehalalel said: Whoever takes four things to
heart will not sin: Where he came from, where he is
going, what will become of him, and who is his judge. (Avos 3:1)
   Where he came from: From a place of darkness,
   Where he is going: To a place of darkness and gloom,
   What will become of him: Dust, worms, and maggots,
   And who is his judge: The King who reigns over kings, the
Holy One, blessed be He.

2. Rabbi Shimon says: He comes from a place of darkness and
returns to a place of darkness. He comes from a putrid drop
[of semen], from a place which the eye cannot see. And what will
become of him? Dust worms and maggots, as it says, *How much
more so man, [who is like] a maggot, and a mortal [who is like] a
worm!* (*Iyov* 25:6).
   Rabbi Eliezer b. Yaakov says: *Man is like a maggot* while he lives,
and a mortal is like a worm when he is dead. *Man is like a maggot*
while he lives, refers to lice, *and a mortal is like a worm* when he is
dead, refers to maggots that infest his body in death.

3. Rabbi Shimon b. Elazar says: Let me compare this to a
parable. A king built and decorated a large palace, but a
[foul-smelling] tannery drain passed through it spilling at its entrance. Every passerby said: "How glorious would this palace be, if
the tannery drain would not pass through it!"
   Man is like this. He exalts himself over other creatures although
a foul-smelling flow emanates from his bowels; imagine how much
more he would exalt himself over other creatures if a flow of fragrant oil, balsam and ointment issued from him!

Rabbi Eliezer's Final Admonition

4. When Rabbi Eliezer fell ill, his disciples visited, sitting before him. "Rabbi," they pleaded, "please teach us one thing [that encompasses all the moral lessons] you have given us."

He told them: "Be mindful of each other's honor, and when you pray, remember before whom you are standing. In this way you will merit life in the World to Come."

Rabbi Elazar b. Azariah said: "We learned five things from Rabbi Eliezer [on his deathbed], which gave us greater delight than anything we learned [from him] during his lifetime."

We asked him [whether the following leather vessels can become ritually unclean]: a round cushion, a ball, a shoemaker's form, an amulet, and torn *tefillin*.[124] He answered: "They can become ritually unclean, and be careful to immerse them in a *mikveh* as they are, [without removing their stuffing], for these are established laws which were conveyed to Moshe on Sinai."

Chapter Twenty

———•◦◉◦•———

Torah for Torah's Sake

1. Rabbi Chaninah, the deputy *Kohen Gadol*, says: One who learns Torah wholeheartedly, [solely for the sake of the

---

124 A leather utensil cannot become *tamei* unless it has a hollow in which something can be placed. The Sages maintain that because the articles listed above have hollows which are permanently filled, it is considered as if they have no hollow and do not become ritually unclean. However if they are ripped open they can become ritually unclean. When they are immersed the stuffing must be removed. Rabbi Eliezer holds since they contain a hollow, although it is filled, they can become *tamei*. He also ruled that the stuffing is regarded as part of the object, and does not have to be removed prior to immersion.

Torah], is freed of anxiety from violence or hunger, from foolish, immoral, lustful, adulterous or trivial thoughts, and from concerns over financial and business matters. For it says, *The precepts of Hashem are just, rejoicing the heart; the command of Hashem is clear making the eyes light up* (*Tehillim* 19:9). But one who does not learn Torah wholeheartedly [exclusively for the sake of the Torah] will suffer anxiety over violence and hunger; will be given to foolish, immoral, lustful, adulterous or trivial thoughts; and will be burdened with worries over financial and business matters. For it says, *[These curses] will be a sign and proof to you and your children forever. When you had plenty of everything, you did not serve Hashem your G-d with happiness and a glad heart. You will therefore serve your enemies which G-d will send against you, in hunger, thirst, nakedness and universal want* (*Devarim* 28:46-48).

In hunger—How so? When you [the Jewish people] are hungry and cannot even find coarse bread, [G-d will send enemies] who demand white bread and prime meat from you.

And in thirst—How so? When you are thirsty and cannot even find a drop of vinegar or beer, [G-d will send enemies] demanding the most exquisite wine in the world from you.

And in nakedness—How so? When you need clothing and cannot even find a woolen or linen shirt, [G-d will send enemies] demanding the finest silks in the world from you.

And universal want—[You will be] in need of a lamp, a knife, and a table.

Another interpretation of, *And universal want:* [You will be] in need of vinegar and salt. This is the origin of the curse people wish [on their enemies]: "Your house should be without salt and vinegar!"

EXPOUNDING VERSES IN *SHIR HASHIRIM*

[Rabbi Chaninah the deputy *Kohen Gadol*] used to expound the verse, *Don't stare at me because I am swarthy, because the sun has darkened me; my mother's sons incited against me. They made me guard the vineyards, my own vineyard I did not guard* (*Shir Hashirim* 1:6).

Don't stare at me because I am swarthy—this refers to the wealthy leaders of Yehudah who threw off the yoke of the Holy One, blessed be He, and brought the domination of foreign rulers down on them.[125]

My mother's sons incited against me—this refers to Moshe who killed the Egyptian. For it says, *When Moshe was grown he went out to his own people, and he saw their hard labor. . . and he looked all around, and when he saw that there was no man [watching], he killed the Egyptian and hid his body in the sand* (*Shemos* 2:11,12).

Why does it say, *he saw that there was no man [watching]*? This teaches that Moshe convened a court of ministering angels and asked them: "Shall I kill this Egyptian?" They replied, "Kill him!" [*He saw that there was no man watching* cannot mean he was afraid of being observed, because] he did not kill the Egyptian with a sword rather he killed him by uttering Hashem's name, as it says, [One of the two men who were fighting said,] "*Do you mean to tell me that you will kill me as you killed the Egyptian?*" the words "tell me" teach that Moshe killed the Egyptian by uttering G-d's name.

My mother's sons incited against me—refers to Dassan and Aviram, [two men who informed against Moshe to Pharaoh, causing him to flee to Midian], as it says, *When Pharaoh heard about the affair, he took steps to have Moshe put to death. Moshe fled from Pharaoh, and ended up in the land of Midian where he was sitting near the well . . . other shepherds came and tried to chase [Yisro's daughters] away. Moshe got up and came to their aid, and watered their sheep* (*Shemos* 2:15). Moshe appeared on the scene and acted as judge. He said to the shepherds: "The accepted custom is that men draw water and women water the animals. Here women draw the water and men water the animals! What a distorted sense of justice you have in this place!" So he got up and came to their aid.

Some say: As long as Moshe remained standing at the mouth of

---

[125] The connection of this segment to the foregoing is the Mishnah in *Avos* 3:6: "If someone throws off the yoke of Torah from himself - the yoke of government is placed upon him."

the well, the water kept surging and rising toward him; when he left, the water flowed back.

[Having saved the girls from their oppressors,] Moshe exclaimed: "Woe is me that I left my people and came to live among non-Jews, [for I surely would have been able to save my people]."

Another interpretation: *My mother's sons incited against me,* refers to [the "mixed multitude" who incited] Yisrael when they made the golden calf. For at first they proclaimed, *We will do and obey all that Hashem has declared* (*Shemos* 24:7); then they changed their mind and said, *This, Yisrael, is your god!* (*Shemos* 32:4).

Another interpretation: *My mother's sons incited against me,* refers to the spies who spread an evil report about the land, causing death to strike Yisrael, as it says, *Your corpses will fall in the desert* (*Bamidbar* 14:29).

They made me guard the vineyards, my own vineyard I did not guard—Said the Holy One, blessed be He: "Who has caused Me to show favor to the idol worshippers? Only Yisrael!"[126] For while Yisrael were despised, pushed around, and roaming [through the wilderness for forty years] the [Canaanite] idolaters enjoyed tranquility.

Another interpretation: *They made me guard the vineyards, my own vineyard I did not guard,* refers to the Jews when they were exiled to Babylonia. The prophets among them urged them to set aside *terumah* offerings and tithes. The Jews answered: ["You don't have to exhort us, we know] we were sent into exile because we did not separate *terumah* and tithes. [You need not] tell us to separate *terumah* and tithes now, [for every G-d-fearing Jew will want to rectify this mistake].

This is the thought behind the verse, *They made me guard the vineyards, my own vineyard I did not guard.*

---

[126] As punishment for accepting the evil report of the spies, B'nei Yisrael had to wander in the desert for forty years, instead of entering Eretz Yisrael immediately. All that time, G-d showed favor to the Canaanite idolaters, granting them peace and tranquility.

GLOSSARY

AGGADAH - Homiletic discourses
AVOS - Fathers, Ethics of the Fathers
B'NEI YISRAEL - Children of Israel
BAMIDBAR - The Book of Numbers
BEIS HAMIKDASH - Holy Temple
BEREISHIS - The Book of Genesis
CHALITZAH - the ceremony whereby a woman whose husband
     left no progeny is released
DEVARIM - The Book of Deuteronomy
DIVREI HAYAMIM - The Book of Chronicles
EICHA - The Book of Lamentations
ERETZ YISRAEL - The Land of Israel
EREV - the day preceding a holiday
GALUS - exile
GEMARA - Talmud
HALACHAH pl. *HALACHOS* - law
HASHEM - God
IYOV - Job
KESUVAH - marriage contract
KOHEIN pl. *KOHANIM* - Priests, descendants of Aaron
KOHEIN GADOL - High Priest
KOHELES - Ecclesiastes
MAMZER - illegitimate child
MELACHIM - The Book of Kings
MIKVEH - ritual immersion pool
MILAH - circumcision
MISHLEI - Proverbs

MISHNAH - compilation of the oral tradition; it also refers to one paragraph of this compilation

MITZVAH pl. *MITZVOS* - commandment

NIDDAH - menstruant woman

PESACH - Passover

SHABBOS - The day of rest - Saturday

SHAVUOS - Festival of Weeks

SHECHINA - Divine Presence

SHEMA - the portion of the Torah containing the declaration of Hashem's unity

SHEMONEH ESREI - the eighteen beracha prayer that we say thrice each day

SHEMOS - The Book of Exodus

SHIR HASHIRIM - Song of Songs

SHOFTIM - The Book of Judges

SUKKOS - Festival of Tabernacles

TAHARAH - ritual purity

TALLIS - prayer shawl

TAMEI - ritually impure

TANACH - Scriptures

TEFILLIN - phylacteries

TEHILLIM Psalms

TESHUVA - REPENTANCE

TUM'AH ritual impurity

VAYIKRA - The Book of Leviticus

YAAKOV - Jacob

YAMIM TOVIM - holidays

YECHEZKEL - Ezekiel

YERUSHALAYIM - Jerusalem

YESHAYAH - Isaiah

YETZER HARA - evil inclination

YIBBUM - levirate marriage where the wife of one who died without progeny, marries his brother

YIRMIYAH - Jeremiah

YISRAEL - Israel

YITZCHOCK - Isaac

YOEL - Joel